Unvaxxed Soul

a post-pandemic spirit journey

gerard-thomas

Authors Note

gerard-thomas is a writer from the West of Ireland and the voice behind the Substack publication The West's Awake, found at westawake.substack.com.

Unvaxxed Soul – a post-pandemic spirit journey is his first book, a memoir. While it grew in part from reflections first shared on The West's Awake, it also marks a new step: a more sustained, intimate exploration of one person's walk across the West of Ireland and into the quieter country of the soul.

He has been writing for around nine years, publishing hundreds of articles that move between current affairs, politics, culture and faith. A recurring thread in his work is the age of digital control—the quiet way screens, data and online systems press in on the inner life, shaping how we think, speak and pray.

His pieces are written in a conversational, closely worked style—but with a clear eye for rhythm, image and line. He leans on story, humour and lived detail as paths into deep questions.

Over 7,000 subscribers now read his work on Substack: a loose gathering of people who still care about conscience, spirit and what it means to stay human. He writes there regularly, with new essays, reflections and updates for readers who wants to follow his writing a little further down the road.

Dedications to:

Vilmute, Jack and Max —mo chlann talamh

Copyright

Copyright © 2025 gerard-thomas

All rights reserved.

ISBN: [9798272545237]

Table of Contents

Authors Note..2

Prologue: Words and me..8

PART 1: SAOIRSE...15

Have you ever considered you might be a cunt?.............................16

The Manager...22

A Screeching Wheel Nut...27

A Mother and Son Sit Down to Talk...35

Saoirse Creatives...43

Interlude: Primroses...48

PART 2: BRIGID...51

A Decision and a Little News...52

A Rendezvous with Aloneness..55

Brigid..60

What Mike Tyson taught me about Spirituality.............................68

The Remnant..73

A Valley of Darkness..80

Thoughts from a Country Hospital...82

A Recovering Masculine..89

A Little Beauty in the Beast..94

One Enchanted Moment..100

   - a short story on healing..100

The Secrets of an Island 112

A Passenger to my Thoughts 118

A Summons to Knock 122

Vaccinating the Blood of Jesus Christ 132

Interlude: My Favourite Word 136

Life on the Road Less Travelled 137

A Stained-glass Window 144

PART 3: SHADOWLANDS 147

A Fork in the Road 148

Lead us not into Temptation 152

Somewhere Else 156

A Dream within a Dream 160

    Outside the Realm 160

    Entering the Realm 162

Grief 165

The Lady of Lough Derravaragh 166

    - a short story on an ancestral pain 166

The Well 191

A Trip to Calvary 193

Brigid and Frankie Go to Hollywood 199

The Wood of the Whispering 203

Divinity between Cell Towers 209

Everybody Knows 214

The Inauthenticity Killer 220

PART 4: THE GREEN MILE 223

I Can't Move..224
    Part 1 224
    Part 2 226
A Random Conversation 228
The Dampened Nettles 230
Track Machines of Intimacy 232
    Part 1 232
    Part 2 236
A Grá Unconditional 241
    - a short story about love 241
At a Snail's Pace..245
The Sun beneath an Apple tree.......................................247
A Herd of Cows Escapes the Matrix...............................248
Bogside Brown Bread. 252
Eclectic Picnic...255
Requiem to Jack and the Hop-Ups 257
Resurrection of a Driver's Licence.................................262
Parting is such Sweet Sorrow..266
Himself and me 269
Epilogue..273
Mo Anam Cara **275**

Prologue: Words and me

Words found me one dark February evening eight years ago while working the night shift—between cigarette breaks and a month-long, throbbing, endless, guilty silence. I was on my knees contemplating the seductive attractiveness of the thinly carpeted office floor. It was a black period, maybe the blackest, but the last shred of something inside me refused to die. Maybe it was a faint, faceless hope. Or, perhaps, even the soothing sedation of grey hopelessness. I didn't know if this hanging thread of a thing was bad or good. Either way, it wouldn't quite let me go.

I got up, sat down, and slowly began to punch out some words on my computer screen—a distraction portal of escape. I can't remember what I typed, and it doesn't really matter, because those first few consonants and vowels began a trail—millions of word-pebbles long now—that signposted a path leading me here. A place I'm more than happy to be, most of the time, and energised by the mystery of where the next twenty thousand words might lead.

Over the last few years, I've written myself out of the factory environment into more inexpensive spaces, freer places. However, I have also penned my way into bad times, pointless arguments, and more than a few cul-de-sacs. It's not been all sweetness and light by any stretch of the imagination. A constant adventure and learning exercise.

Words are about the only thing I have consistently shown up for over these past eight years—which isn't much of a statement, but isn't nothing, I guess. Over time, little by little, they've spoon-fed me puddles of tears and occasional puddings of laugh-out-loud hilarity—exposing wounds, strengths, and some sort of healing too.

Of course, in the beginning, I had no idea what I was doing—or precisely what these innocuous-looking rascals were doing to me. They were stirring something, though. At times deep and at times frivolously shallow. You might say we began a stumbling walk, then a slow, awkward dance together. A companionship and rhythm developed. Soon enough, I fell in love with them completely—a lover of sorts, but one I frequently fall out with too. But I can't imagine ever giving up on them, because they speak to me when no one else can reach me.

Along the way, we've bumped into the curious sights and sounds of a world losing its mind. Together, carefully jotting down each eruption of new oddness before shuffling along to the next outbreak. Somewhat comforted by the notion that while I might be a little unhinged at times, the world around me seems to be completely losing the fucking plot altogether.

Examining the lights and shadows of earthly things brought me back to an examination of the lights and shadows within me. Not the prettiest of sights, but shouldn't have been a surprise given how I began the journey—on my knees on a factory floor—yet somehow it was a great surprise indeed.

Through words, I stumbled upon a voice within, I suppose. A murmur I couldn't quite decipher consistently or understand without the aid of a keyboard. The signal is still somewhat intermittent, but sometimes, if I still myself long enough, I can hear the echo of this voice calling from the depths of me.

I'm not sure when traces of my soul first began the annoying habit of elbowing into my written conversations to dot some i's and cross a few t's. Maybe always. She shows up unexpectedly, and rarely in a paragraph you'd expect a teaspoon of femininity to be integral. That's another thing—I've always considered my soul a she for some reason. Moving within like a powerful softness, melting walls of harsh male granite and a few jagged edges as she flows by.

At times, this soul of mine—or anam, as we say here in Ireland—resonates strangely, a literary editor not concerned a jot with plotlines, deadlines, dense intellectual thinking, or even facts and the pursuit of narratives of the day. Inconveniently, she doesn't make apparitions in that fashion at all, at all.

I only know the anam is present when I become obsessed with a sentence.

It is a glorious self-indulgence to describe myself as a writer, I know. But it is a label that rather suits my lifestyle, at any rate. In a recent piece, I referenced a couple of appearances I made at the District Court in Ireland. On one of these occasions I was forced to engage the inexpensive legal services of Me, Myself & I, Incorporated. At the outset, the judge enquired of me my current occupation—to which I replied, rather magnificently, 'I'm a writer.' You know, just in case he might have mistaken me for any old run-of-the-mill legal expert versed in the finer points of the Road Traffic Act, 1961.

His reaction to the 'writer' designation was quite amusing, but one I've encountered before on my travels—a startled little pause of breath and then narrowing of the eyes—before continuing on as if I hadn't said the blasphemous word aloud at all. As if someone equal parts mad and dangerous, and quite possibly intoxicated by delusions of inner freedom, had just stumbled into his domain. Best for all concerned to ignore and move on.

However, the moment was a test of me in a way. Away from the safety blanket of a twelve-inch laptop screen, does the word breathe in me out in the world—and how about in front of a packed public gallery, lawyers, and a dozen cops looking on? Indeed, do I feel the echo of it on the dark nights, staring at my own reflection in some frozen puddle on the side of a road?

Well, happily, the short answer seems to be yes.

In fact, during this scoundrels-only court conclave, the word massaged my shoulders, unfurrowed my brow, and brushed a strengthening and comfortable smile across my face. On the occasions when I'm suddenly and diligently invested in the outcome of a sentence, the same recurring question keeps surfacing in my mind. The question is never about how the sentence reads, but about something else entirely.

'How does that sound?'

Once the eyes have performed a preliminary check, the voice of my mind takes over, repeating the words, again and again, offering tweaks, adjustments of placement, and frank criticism.

'And how does that sound?'

'No.'

'And now?'

'Fuckin' worse.'

'Try it again now.'

'You fuckin' try it again instead.'

'OK, one more time.'

On and on, until the questions and question marks evaporate and are replaced with the gentle tingling of an emotion. A true emotion. When the final word drops into place, it clicks open a combination lock to somewhere else—perhaps only for a moment or two, but long enough to absorb the small truth uncovered and a sense that the final word unpicking it was worth the wait. Worth the effort. The aroma of madness and pain around the process then becomes part of the prize.

It's all very exhausting, which is why I invest sparingly in sentences. I need to make a little go a long way, or else I'd never get anything published—or ever stop talking to myself. The key point here is that my philosophy on words is that they are meant not to be read but spoken a little tipsily in the head. Like a good conversation you might open up to after a few pints of Guinness in the pub but can't quite remember in the morning. Other than a vague notion it sang to a part of your soul not often revealed or brought out to play.

The final judge and jury of the voice-writing is the voice in my mind, simultaneously speaking and feeling the words, and this voice is often chiding me with the demand to find a few precise ones to help unshackle the gates to my soul.

Curiously, the written pieces of my own still gently pulsing are those where my trusty old editor had her firm hand steering the tiller. Everyone should find time to give voice to their voice, now and again, I think. For when you hone the words and a voice emerges from the murmur, it is the rarest and truest of friends: exposing weaknesses and offering stern words of warning to tackle them, while also whispering guidance, good humour, and healing into an unvaxxed soul. And we all have common access to one of those, I believe. .

Words swirl and circulate through my veins now, replacing the alcohol that once scented my bloodstream—bringing with them the same intermittent highs and lows, and some of the same dangers too. I guess, though, my scribblings are where I now build my house of prayer. My solitude and some sanctity. It is in the quiet, silent spaces between one phrase and the next that I have tripped over forgotten joys and old, buried sadnesses and mined a paragraph to keep me going.

The promise of these happenings guides me on the sleepless nights when speeding down a motorway at a pace matching my latest frantic worry and obsessive thought. Or while trundling down some grassy laneway wrestling with a fragment of my shadow; trying to shadow-box the shard into submission and, much later, into some sort of integration with my spirit.

My spirit's path behind is shovelled and spaded with words, and they seem destined to provide the foundation stones of my journey ahead too—finding them, lump-hammering them, and chiselling them down into place. Searching for a spark which—like cruising into an unexpected flicker of moonlight on a cloud-filled night—will hit me, and chase a trouble away or an understanding into being. A tiny new creation of myself, with a new word arrangement to concrete the dawning into day.

Unfortunately, the further away I get from each typed word, the further too I slope away from encountering any faint whispers of divinity in me. So, I can't afford to step away from them for too long or I'll lose myself again.

Thankfully, a series of keystrokes has always shown up, somehow or some way, to jerk me off the floor, dust me down and send me on my way again. At times, greeting me like an old soul-friend; at others knifing me through the gut like a pure-bred cunt.

Two decisions have shaped the current path of my life. Two questions, really. Questions where the correct answers for me were a rhyming couplet of nays. No to another creamy pint of black gold, and no to the prescribed serum of our times. This is not a book detailing the minutiae of those personal decisions, but rather where they led me. To an alone-filled, forgotten boreen where a slow stripping away of the outer structures and people in my world began to occur.

After a number of years tinkering away with these meanderings of mine in print, I cannot escape the fact that these are almost entirely spiritual tinkerings now. A man searching for the guiding voice within to signpost a way to more regular sit-downs with his anam-croí—soul-heart. An experimental journey, you might say.

I find things, I lose things, and find them again. Lessons learned, mistakes remade—the same lesson in need of re-learning, over and over. Battling to become defined by my strengths rather than my weaknesses. One of God's most impatient typists and weakest spellers in the class—a man filled with missing commas, abrupt full stops, and inexplicable grammatical errors, yet hopeful still of finding one perfect sentence within himself.

What follows is a series of personal episodes—recorded over the last four years—on the hunt for that sentence. So, in a certain sense, I bid you farewell now. Hopefully we'll catch up again close to the finish line. In the meantime, as we say in the West of Ireland, may the road rise up to meet you.

PART 1: SAOIRSE

Have you ever considered you might be a cunt?

Settle down there now, settle down. Risky title, I know. I try to avoid overuse of foul language, but I do like to fleck it in, here and there, as a reminder that we're somewhat alive, well, and still kicking here in the West of Ireland. I'm especially careful with regard to this borderline word rhyming with 'hunt'.

Yet the word was once in common Irish usage, and I have a love story of sorts to tell about it, if you have time to listen. Ah, risk and love—a pair of delinquencies I can't quite shake from my soul's essence.

Now, I'm not sorry for cunt's slow linguistic demise—although it's a word as commonly used in Ireland by men addressing other men as it is when flung in the general direction of the fairer sex. During my teenage experiences, a cunt was a cunt—and you couldn't miss one when you saw him.

In 1980s Ireland, the most important day of the week in the rural village pub scene, from an economic standpoint, was Friday—because Friday was the day those of suitable agedness received their old-age pension from the state and local post office. During the summers of '88 and '89, my job in the family pub business was to man the bar counter from 10:30 am until 6 pm, when my father finished work at his regular job.

The post office was about fifty or sixty yards to the right of our rented pub—a strategic advantage over our competition on pension day—and a butcher's shop adjoined us on the left-hand side. Friday mornings were usually busy in the village. On most fine, sunny mornings, I'd cycle or walk to work, and on a Friday there'd be three or four of those old High Nelly bicycles and a couple of Ford Hunters queued up outside, the bikes at rest, decorating the front wall of the pub.

A small crowd of old bucks would be huddled in front of the butcher's shop—wallets temporarily topped up with the weekly pension—gossiping good-humouredly. Lightly swinging white plastic bags of lamb cutlets or stewing beef in the breeze, the meat to be added to a feed of boiled potatoes later in the day. Or for some, the day after that, if the drinking activities of the morning got the better of them.

By lunchtime, the high stools at the counter would be lined with twelve or thirteen old fellas lamenting the tragedy of living in a country no longer stopping as often to drink during the day. A line of philosophical thinking leading them to believe that a country no longer pausing to sip on a glass of stout might soon contemplate stopping to sit down and think altogether.

By three o'clock, the front bar often cleared out as daughters-in-law docked in to collect the patriarchs of the local family farms and deposit the bikes in the boot of a car or the back of an old jeep. The bachelors would linger a while longer and pocket twenty Sweet Afton cigarettes and tiny naggin bottles of Powers whiskey for the road ahead—shooting off on their High Nellies, secure in the knowledge that swearing off women was entirely the correct decision for men with a fondness for drink, a small cottage, twenty acres of land, and only a few cattle and sheep.

It was in this dead zone between the early pension-day traffic and the beginning of the weekend proper, a few hours later, that an old alcoholic, John, used to land into us. His morning spent in another public house, but once his welcome was worn out there he'd chance his arm and come into our place—safe in the knowledge that the innate decency of my father would ensure that, while he too would ask him to leave the premises at a certain point during the evening, he'd also throw John's bike in the back of his red council jeep and deposit him safely home to his cottage and fields of ewe hoggets.

Anyway, on this day—the one lodged in my memory—John o' the Hill, as we used to call him, arrived into an empty front bar. I suspect he liked to find it that way more often than he didn't. The pain of his addiction was writ large on his features. He'd often order a shot of dark rum and a bottle of Guinness together as a starter. John could curse you into oblivion, but at other times also reveal the most intimate details about himself and the mistakes he'd made in his life. The hard, weather-beaten coarseness of his face and lifestyle disguised deep, almost feminine, traces of softness.

I still remember the redness of the skin around his eyes and also the painful veiny reds ebbing in and flowing out of the white of his eyes on the bad days. He was small and handsome in an earlier time and place, no doubt about it; but a gruelling life dedicated to the drink and the land had much of the beauty bet out of him.

You might stumble upon anything or nothing in his deep blue eyes—occasionally a tranquillised nothingness, other times sadness, wild joy, tenderness—and sometimes, like on this fine summer's day, he might be fighting the demons and the darkness within.

John didn't seem much in the mood for conversation on this pension day, and he spent a good thirty or forty minutes looking me up and down as I pottered about behind the counter. Even so, I could sense bad energy and unpleasant vibrations. I was both frightened and attracted to it, if the truth be known. John o' the Hill was staring at me like he had something harsh and nasty to say about my being. Yet most conversation starters were met only with a grunt in reply. After a time, he moved on to swamping pints of beer and, at one point, I eyed that the ring of froth on the inside of his pint glass was inching dangerously close to empty.

'Will I stick on another pint of Smithwick's for you there, John?' I enquired, innocently enough—but not settled on whether I wanted him to stay or go.

He nodded his head up and down, but there was a hint of malevolence and hatred in his eyes. He looked at me—looked through me, really—and then spoke, softly but with an undoubted sliver of animosity directed towards me and self-loathing pulsing back into himself.

'Young fella, have you ever considered that you might be a cunt—a real bad one, like?'

The question, and the wave of negativity lacing it, hit me like a bolt from the blue and pierced past my non-existent teenage defences straight to my darkness. For yes—absolutely yes indeed—I had considered, and spent quite an amount of my youth (and much later on still) contemplating this very question. And of just how big of one I might well turn out to be in the end, when the singing and dancing of my life was finally complete. John's shadow had thrown a poisoned dart and hit bullseye on my own.

Curiously, though, the dangerous question had found a safe space in which to be considered. I was drawn in and not repulsed. Now, I can't for the life of me remember my exact response—or even if I responded to the enquiry in kind—but the black question broke the ice between us on this particular pension day.

Strangely—or maybe not strangely at all—we spent the next window of time pondering the darkness of ourselves together. Sometimes with words and sometimes with silences.

His tongue unknotted itself and he confessed he had been in love once with a nurse. He spoke of the intimate details of her—not of beauty or brains, but of the way she held a brush and swept the floor; the way she moved, gliding across the neighbouring fields, herding cattle. It was the kind of intimate knowing I yearned for too. Laughter, merriment, and love danced to life in his eyes as he spoke of her.

'What happened—why didn't you marry her?' I blurted out, impatient for a happy ending, though I knew none was coming.

'Sure, I never told her. I could never let her marry a cunt like me.'

More heavy silence fell. I repeated his last sentence in my head and tried to conjure up an image of the woman in my mind's eye. I could feel the dark power of the words and the truth he'd just spoken.

'I could never let her marry a cunt like me.'

Surprisingly, they resonated deeply within me—but only much later would I piece together the exact reason why. I began to nod my head slowly at his predicament and logic, but wasn't quite willing to relinquish the hope of one day unearthing a different wisdom and different ending.

Soon, the door of the front bar brushed open and a new customer entered our private domain, and our whispered confessional came to an abrupt halt. I felt sorry for John o' the Hill that afternoon and, in a way, felt sorry for myself too. Two odd cunts in a village of even pricks.

I often wonder, do the secret inhabitants of power and greed, driving society's coldest narratives with such surety, ever stop to ask themselves the specific question that so consumed John o' the Hill that pension-day afternoon? Have they explored where the light ends and the darkness begins inside themselves—the winding roads and meandering pathways in and out of it? Probably not too deeply, if at all, I'd suppose. And can you hope to amount to anything much—or true—without facing down these possibilities and probabilities within?

'Have you ever considered that you might be a cunt—a real bad one, like?'

Some folks consider it too much. And yet more, not nearly enough.

The Manager

I catch glimpses of John staring silently back at me from the mirror. The older I get, the more often I see him there. Smiling that bashful, wry smile of his and puffing away on a filterless Sweet Afton. A bachelor—he grew older as we grew up in the home-house, more brother than uncle.

The nineteen-eighties description of him would've been that he was odd, with the poor nerves at him the whole time. Chain-smoking cigarettes and drinking endless streams of sugared tea. Quiet as a church mouse. I note that I chain-smoke, drink from the same stream of sugared tea, and haven't been saying too much lately. He smiles, winks back at me from the mirror, and puts the spare hand out to cadge a fag for later, God rest him.

The nineteen-nineties medicated his poetry of oddness and nerves into the soulless phraseology of the science wizards, and so terms like paranoid schizophrenia began popping up in conversation. Injecting tranquillised stillness while gradually removing the life force from behind his beautiful blue eyes, bit by bit.

He was an angel, of course, but as my mother would comment, you needed to be a feckin' martyr to live with him. I am tempted to say he hadn't much of a life but, again, the older I get, the more untruth I find in that thought stream. Back in the mirror, I can see we are both men of the night and secretly smiling to ourselves. As time flies by, I am just beginning to dig into myself and discover a lot of people live there.

Everyone called him The Manager, but no one knew why exactly. An irony, perhaps. He had twenty-eight acres of land in three parcels scattered around the village, and when he moved in with us, my father began farming the land alongside him.

At one time, The Manager lived and managed on his own, but an episode with a cigarette butt and flaming bed put an end to his bachelor living. Cattle and sheep were at ease in his company. On more than one occasion, I'd find one or the other in his run-down bungalow front kitchen mooching around while he was brewing the tea. He'd spend hours sitting on his small front porch smoking, drinking tay, and pacing. Occasionally, slapping himself across the forehead and having mighty conversations with himself out loud. I've caught myself doing similar on one or two occasions while driving the back-roads at night.

I consider him afresh tonight as I watch the number of empty mugs mount on the back-kitchen windowsill of my own house. I glance up at the black sky, and wait for some moonlight to break through the carpet of cloud so that I might feel something and sit down and write about it in peace.

Back when the school holidays kicked in and the first available stretch of good weather emerged, my old man always paired John and myself together to perform the big day-to-day summertime chores of a small breathing farm—the Clare man, like most Clare folk, a wild optimist. I remember a day saving the turf with John. The bog ritual involved an early morning dumping off on the bog road by my father on his way to work in the County Council and collection in the evening on the return leg home—armed with his apology of cheeseburgers and chips.

Most of the time, I'd spend as much of the day exploring the bog and the depths of the different bog holes as doing the actual manual labour of lifting sods of turf. After the obligatory hour of throwing shapes at the lines of never-ending brown sausage rolls in front of us, the two of us would stretch out on some bank of beaten-down heather, smoking. Me, drinking gulps from a big bottle of TK red lemonade, and him slurping tea from a flask cup. I'd often have a paperback book or some comics stashed away somewhere on my person and lay back to read.

Sometimes, if Uncle John wasn't too agitated with his nerves, he'd get relaxed enough from smoking and drinking tea to forget I was there and start talking to himself. He was funny, articulate, and animated in these unconscious, full-blown conversations. Like a different man altogether. Then, of course, he'd catch you looking at him, and his self-consciousness would return in an instant. The words dying suddenly on the bog breeze, frightened and vanished away.

His was a voice, a sod of turf, trapped on the wrong bank in the bog, you might say. So delicate and yet so dangerous too. We never found the right key to unlock his true voice. And sometimes you just don't find it, I guess. Perhaps my mind is playing tricks, but odd characters were falling out of the hawthorn bushes in most Irish villages of the nineteen-eighties. Or so it seemed.

Our little townland had about fifteen houses, and at least five of those households were taken up with a category of person you don't hear of anymore: confirmed bachelors. They were, one and all, various flavours of odd. If mental health had a business model back then, it came in the form of a threat to dissuade potential users of it. Families would endure all forms of mental anguish to avoid entrusting a loved one to the confines of the Irish mental health system. For in the West of Ireland, the system meant spending time in a mental hospital. And having a family member located, for any period of time, in a facility such as this was a label that stuck to a whole family.

'Be careful, or you'll end up in Ballinasloe like The Manager.'

It was a brutal system, and our family felt the full force of its limitations with regard to our uncle. Yet poverty, or necessity, is indeed the mother of invention. The lack of resources forced communities to find a little elbow room for the differing colours in the rainbow of eccentricities surrounding them. The village understood my uncle and weren't afraid of him, for he presented no physical threat. But if he ran out of cigarettes, it was not uncommon for us to find out the following morning that he'd traipsed down into the village at 2 am, banging down the door of one of the local shops in search of his next smoke.

People somehow found a way to tolerate this occasional inconvenience, by and large, because they knew we were doing our best. And by we, I mean my mother. Towns and villages were forced, through necessity, to be robust enough to cope.

It's the fortunate family that isn't hit with mental health issues of one type or another. In my own exposure to it in my family, lifelong mental illness is almost banal, such is the almost imperceptible trace of its progression. The most noticeable changes are often visible in the people closest to the sufferer rather than in the sufferer themselves. My uncle had a certain obliviousness to his own state. People dealing with these types of people often convince themselves they are above and beyond the reaches of its outstretched arms. My experience is that they most certainly are not.

I don't know the answers, even sitting here now, but I know it didn't happen overnight or even over a specific series of them. The progression was much slower. I can't quite place a time and date as to when these episodes, and others, turned from the almost silly, funny anecdote of the momentarily forgetful to the roars of tortured anguish of the perpetually cursed.

But they did.

All I can say for certain is that it was the woman of the house who bore the deepest and most long-lasting scars. The person that bent the most to accommodate, at some point, struggled to stand fully upright. The decision to remove someone from your home for the overall well-being of the household is one of the hardest ones a family in these circumstances has to make. And I suppose the beauty and tragedy of Ireland back then is that many homes couldn't, or wouldn't, bring themselves to make it. Call it empathy, sympathy, guilt, or some other emotion affiliated with caring too much. We couldn't, and the hidden price of it was not small.

At what point were we a family that started hiding bread and tea bags in the washing machine at night?

And then, at what point after were we tragically unaware of hanging freshly washed, tea-stained jeans and the odd geansaí wetted by bread dough on the clothesline?

I don't know.

Yet I didn't realise how much I loved him until tonight; if I hadn't grown up with The Manager, there'd be a stranger looking back at me in the mirror—a part of me I'd never truly understand.

A Screeching Wheel Nut

My father's people sprang out of the Burren rocks around Lisdoonvarna and Kilfenora in County Clare before scattering along a stretch of coastal wildness that extends from Doolin down as far as Lahinch. I was reminded of them all during the past week as I set about putting some meat on the bones of a creatives' retreat in West Clare—a gathering of creatively non-compliant ne'er-do-wells like myself, between you, me, and the wall.

My idea—a black sheep's ball—to take place just weeks after the white sheep have reopened the gates to the untamed fields (and pubs, restaurants, and coffee shops too). Two years of brutal darkness are ending and the doors of freedom, or Saoirse in the native tongue, have cracked open an inch or two. My instinct is to rip doors like this off their hinges for fear any of the clever fools class get the daft notion to try and close them again. The question and answer as to why I am organising this little shindig is probably similar to why I write.

I travelled down last Thursday to check out a few venues while listening, with increasing intent, to the noise that a screeching wheel nut was making from my right front tyre. It was threatening to abort the mission halfway up the winding Corkscrew Hill, a few miles outside Ballyvaughan.

On other escapades up this hill, thoughts usually centre around my father and something that happened to him on this patch of road over fifty years ago now. As the story goes, when he was fifteen or sixteen, he lost half an ear in a motorbike accident on top of the Corkscrew. The curiosity is not the incident itself but rather how the information came into my possession. I only heard about this heirloom of family history about ten years ago outside a funeral parlour in Limerick. I was smoking a cigarette and stood beside an uncomfortably suited man hanging out of one as well. He was about my father's age—which is to say about twenty years or so older than myself.

'Which one of the O'Neills are you—Gerry's or MJ's lad?'

'Gerry's—and another Gerry as well,' I offered by way of explanation and introduction as I shook his hand.

'I was good buddies with Gerry when we were young lads. I was with him the night he lost the ear.'

I pretended I knew what the hell he was talking about and nodded.

'Ah Jaysus, we were going full tilt down the Corkscrew from the Spa (Lisdoonvarna) and toppled over on top of our heads and sure his ear got jammed in the bike chain.'

They must have managed to sew it back on again, I thought to myself, because even as dopey and distracted as I am and was—I'd have noticed growing up with a one-eared father.

'I picked it up off the ground—blood everywhere there was,' and then, in a conspiratorial whisper, he added:

'Of course now, drink was taken.'

I did the maths in my head—it would have been about 1966 or 1967, I supposed. I'd have been surprised if there wasn't drink taken given the attitudes and mores of those times. My father arrived over as we were discussing this.

'Ah yeah—the ear,' he said, smiling, as he involuntarily raised his hand to touch the offending appendage in question.

I'm relating this flick of a tale to indicate we are the type of family where fundamental things or events are sometimes never spoken about—whether that be a missing ear or a fella with notions about writing. We still manage to rub along, as my father's family are mostly doers. They are happiest doing things with you or for you, rather than engaging in deep explorations of the soul over the dinner table. I find them refreshing to be around sometimes, as I'm more of a thinker than a doer.

When I eventually arrived into Doolin, I was met by my aunt in the foyer of one of the local hotels. She and her husband have been running the same pub and eatery in Doolin for forty years and more. When I started laying out my plans about the Saoirse creatives' weekend, I had to reveal how the hell I knew any creative people in the first place. I admitted to partaking in a bit of writing like a junkie might confess to snorting the odd line of cocaine. I was a bit awkward about it, to say the least.

'Isn't that just marvellous now,' she said.

'Ah sure, it helps keep the mind focused on something else, I guess'—the 'else' being alcohol.

'You seem a bit more together the last few times I've met you. How long since you gave up the sauce?'

'You'll laugh at this now because usually alcoholics know to the second when they quit. But it's either five or six years—the first week of January.'

'Was it hard?'

'Well, it's a bit like this: it took me ten years to make the decision, and it took less than an hour to realise it was the right one after I went to an AA meeting.'

'Ah sure, some people just reach their quota of drink earlier than expected.'

A lovely way of putting it that appealed to my ear—lovelier than I deserved, probably. So, I guess we are that type of family on the father's side. A family where we keep some things to ourselves, but if one of us shows up out of the big blue yonder after a couple of years of radio silence, we're met with kindness and immediate, practical help—as was the case with organising this retreat.

I spent a lovely afternoon with my aunt driving through the village—first up to the Doolin Cave and then the community centre. My aunt helpfully pointed out B&Bs that would be open, slowing down to allow me to snatch pictures of the signs and save me the effort of committing the names and numbers to a notepad.

Finally, we passed the Fitz's B&B as we cruised back into Doolin village. Jimmy Fitz was a friend I made in my teenage years and who worked alongside me in my aunt's pub during the early nineties. A farmer now, and his family run a thriving bed-and-breakfast business too. Many's the night we spent drinking and laughing in McDermott's and around the small towns of County Clare.

'You'd better call into Jim—the pick-up is parked at the side there. He's home.'

I arrived into the back kitchen and let out a roar for him.

'Jim… anyone home?'

I repeated the call five or six times more before I heard a stirring somewhere within.

'Ah you fuckin' Jesus cunt, will you stop roaring—what are you doing in Doolin?'

I couldn't help but laugh at the shock of blue language, and then explained. We spent a happy fifteen minutes reminiscing and I filled him in on the retreat—to which he said:

'Why the fuck would you be doing something like that?'

I arrived back out to the aunt's car still chuckling.

'Well, Jim is still Jim,' I said, looking at her.

'If we could only get him to stop cursing, he'd have no problem getting a woman for himself. He's a heart of gold, you know.'

I knew very well.

'Sure he wouldn't be Jim without the fuckin' and blindin', I suppose.'

Indeed, he's quite a shock to the system for the first thirty minutes after you meet him. Although once you settle into the rhythm of his west Clare speech patterns, you quickly get used to it and enjoy the musicality. All the women in our family are stone-mad about him—from thirty up to the mid-sixties age range—and spend a great deal of time fondly chattering about him too. He'd be the type who, if you happened to lose an ear on the side of the Corkscrew Hill, would pick it and you up off the ground, and go banging down the door of a stranger's house for help.

'Will you put this fuckin' thing in a glass with some ice—this fucker out here is after losing his ear; we need to try and save it for the cunt.'

After the whistle-stop tour of Doolin, my aunt brought me back to her home-house for a feed of fried eggs and rashers. We spent an hour going through all the old Doolin characters that were part of its patchwork quilt in the 1990s. Sadly, many have passed on to the other world.

One was still alive, though. A farmer and kind of labourer called Johnny. Johnny was a rip-roaring alcoholic but was—and I have no doubt about this—a genius. You could find him talking about the opening moves from game three or four of the world chess championship of 1972 between Bobby Fischer and Boris Spassky in the middle of a Tuesday afternoon. I was particularly drawn to his vocabulary. I have only met two or three other people who could switch gears, vocabulary-wise, like he could. He could reduce or expand his vocabulary and phraseology at will, depending on the type of individual he was drawn into conversing with on a subject.

Occasionally, when he was drunk, he would let fly with it—and it was a sight to behold. When the drink got a bad hold of him, though, it was difficult to make out a word he was saying—lost as he was in a world of conversation that only he understood. Plenty of intelligent people stayed clear of him when he was in full flow for the simple reason that he made them feel inferior. This was never intentional—and that was one of the reasons I liked him so much. A lot of us just weren't smart enough to carry a conversation with him. Not one that would keep him engaged for more than five minutes anyway.

Back then, in the pre-internet age, he could casually and effortlessly talk profoundly on a wide variety of subjects—leaving you in no doubt that you were in the presence of someone with a deep wisdom but also a wicked sense of humour. I often wondered if it was his brains that made him drink—just to get relief from the river of thoughts. He sometimes reminded me of an agrarian George Best. The whole village used to pray for him to give up the sauce. I was thankful to find out he did conquer that demon.

I know from experience that there are many different types of alcoholic. I was the binge-drinking kind—where there'd sometimes be big gaps between two or three days of frenzied drinking sessions. Enough time off to half convince yourself you didn't have a problem. Johnny was a different type—or at least he was during the period I spent working down there.

Sometimes, when you'd land a pint or a whiskey in front of him you could see the pain chiselled on his face just trying to drink the first pint or two. Tears would well up in his eyes and it required pure focus just to get the liquid down his throat—until he'd have four or five and find some balance and relief. Drinking eased the pain a touch, but as we all find out eventually, the relief it offers is shorter and shorter-lived.

We spoke fondly of Johnny and his sobriety for a while more until my uncle piped up again.

'Did I tell you about the time the nieces brought him down to the house after they installed Alexa for the first time?' My uncle got into a fit of laughter.

'the niece says to Johnny, "You can ask it anything, Johnny, and it just goes off and gets the answer from the internet."'

"Alexa—could you go off there now and ascertain for me exactly how much money Liam Feeney has managed to accumulate during his lifetime. Good woman."

At the time of writing, Alexa is still looking for the answer.

Later, as I drove home, the phone rang about ten miles from Tuam. It was the old man. Ah—the aunt has rung him, I thought, as I hadn't spoken to him in a good while.

'I hear you're running a bit of a festival down in Doolin. Do you need anything from the pub? We can take tables and chairs from the function room. Sure we'll drop them down in the van the week before if you like?'

I smiled.

The only person to never ask why.

A Mother and Son Sit Down to Talk

Regular visitors to my virtual village on Substack are well aware that my little literary homestead is located at the end of a winding, meandering laneway. Quite often, out walking together, I have difficulty charting the course back home. The trail that leads there is frequently overgrown with thickets, brambles, and changeable weather—with the occasional overhanging crab-apple tree or hawthorn bush thrown in the way for good measure.

When nature or myth imagery occasionally consumes my imagination, it's no pointer to some grand intellectual pedigree, but merely a sign that my mother's clan are of the land—and that I grew up roaming the hedgerowed fields of her people.

I learned a lot about the night and moonlight in my early youth. I understood I came alive by the excitement of it—the unknown quantity and mysteriousness of it. My most treasured memories are of midnight feasts with my childhood best friend, or comharsa béal dorais in Irish.

In those days, all telecommunication appliances shut down between 11.30 pm and midnight. So, once my parents and my friend's widowed dad fell asleep, we'd get to work.

Ingredients for a midnight feast?

Homemade brown soda bread, a block of Calvita cheese, thick slices of butcher's ham, scallions, marmalade, jam, onions, tomatoes. Once, we even managed to boil some eggs early in the day before smuggling them out into the night. The only objective, each night, was to invent a new kind of sandwich—which basically meant accumulating as many different items as possible and jamming them between two roughly hewn slices of bread.

We'd then sit on the side of a ditch, in a field beside his house, and plot methods of lassoing two of that farmer's three donkeys. Or plan tree houses. Or gather material for bonfires and rafts. And always—but always—read comic books. There's nothing quite like reading The Beano or The Dandy by torchlight between mouthfuls of ham, cheese, and marmalade. Trust me on that.

People often look back with the benefit of hindsight and fully appreciate certain aspects of childhood. But not us—we knew, in those moments of adventure, what it meant to be alive. Alive, awake, and unspooked by the darkness. Maybe a little too unspooked…

However, nothing lasts forever—the good or the bad. A final goodbye to a person, a place, or a midnight feast often never occurs. Life rarely signposts that your last happy meal was your last happy meal. For us, the end came through carelessness and the hypnotic trance of Caer Ibormeith and the otherworld—Caer, goddess of sleep and the love in Aengus Óg's dreams.

Across the main road from my house, and adjacent to my neighbour's home, lay the schoolhouse. It was the week before summer holidays and, unbeknownst to our sleeping selves, we had become objects of fun. The early school bus had stopped and beeped a few honks of the horn, but to no avail in stirring the two reposing faerie giants—collapsed in a heap asleep on top of a ditch by the main road for all and sundry to see.

Eventually, my mother was summoned, and a small crowd had gathered at the boundary wall of the schoolyard to gawk and whistle—a mocking derision that knocked hard on our confidence, or certainly mine. So much so, there never was another midnight feast or night of reckless glory unlocking the mysteries of the moonlight. A joint, unspoken decision made between us, I guess.

The recently past season of Omicron brought a gift of sorts—a slight opening of minds among people not currently on my side of the ditch on a certain matter. In a weird way, the white sheep and the blacker ones are feeling the same emotion, I believe: a gnawing sensation of being cheated—although for vastly differing reasons.

Many of my mother's age-stamp feel they were sold a dud; particularly with this third, non-trinity booster. A wave of 'flu-like symptoms' still sweeps the country. A rehashed sales job and a set of warning signals kick into full media swing—in neon ticker-tape flashing across all electronic devices. Suffice to say, the current marketing drive is falling short and old purchasers are not buying it hook, line, and sinker as before.

How do I know this?

Well, there are anecdotal clues all around, so allow me to relate a personal one. The mother of my youth is still, thankfully, around to be the mother of my middle age. By New Year's Day, a majority portion of my family—and extended family—had fallen foul to the sweet seductions of that fifteenth letter of the Greek alphabet. So, my triple-vaxxed mother summoned her vax-free eldest son for an emergency coronavirus summit. A jabbing contest commenced—one that was new, but ancient as well.

'Sit down,' she said.

'No better man,' says I.

Then she looked at me—for a minute—like she was observing me at an angle she hadn't quite seen before. A mixture of curiosity, doubt, annoyance, and just a little touch of wonder around the corners of her eyes. And then she spoke.

'I want to tell you something. I'm only gonna say this once now. I'm thinking you might be on to something. If there's another jab, I'm not sure I'm gonna take it… stop smiling… it had nothing to do with you… don't be thinking it had anything to do with you now.'

Even better for my long-term mental health, I thought, if it hadn't. Best say nothing. So, I gave this news time to settle and idly glanced around the room until my eyes fixed on the kitchen table and the biography of Charlie Haughey—the most infamous political leader in our post-independence history. The volume looked well thumbed.

'How are you getting on with Charlie?'

'Did you know his secondary school year sat the first ever Leaving Cert in Ireland, and he came first, and got top marks in UCD?' she replied in a vaguely accusatory manner, her mind still razor sharp.

Like she had reared a son who'd been hiding Charlie's Irish and Mathematics results under my mattress all these years. I should add that I grew up in a household where Garret FitzGerald—a politician of a different persuasion—was the only show in town, and Charlie Haughey was… well, Charlie. After this attempted distraction, she steered me back on track.

'Why?'

'Why what?' I said.

'Why didn't you do it? Were you not worried you'd get it and give it to me?' she asked.

Her tone was a mixture of a little hurt—which I was well familiar with on this subject and others—but now a little genuine curiosity shone through too.

It's at times like this I fully understand that no one really listens to me anymore—or maybe ever. For we've had many, many conversations on the subject. Too many. But her ears were genuinely pricked now for the first time.

'Well, believe it or not, I'd like to keep you alive for the next fifteen years and not the next fifteen minutes—and no one has been able to convince me that vaccinating me, my kids, and everyone around you is the best way of keeping you alive and them safe.'

She liked the fifteen years bit, I could tell.

We fell into an easy silence, as we often do, as she puffed on a cigarette. I forgot to mention—you're gonna fucking need SEAL Team One to take this woman out—jabbed or unjabbed. We switched subjects again.

'Did you buy yourself any books for Christmas?' she asked.

'I did—an audiobook by Robert Kennedy Jr, Bobby's son.'

Now, I should mention, we'd have been the type of 1980s rug-rats reared staring up at a picture of the Sacred Heart of Jesus and a photo of JFK either side of the mantelpiece—in case, God forbid, we started confusing ourselves with Protestants (especially with all the soccer we were playing over in the schoolyard).

'What's the book called? Could I set it up on the iPad?'

One of the first pandemic purchases we made for her was an iPad. Many hours of screeching and roaring later, the two of us had managed to get through a crash course in Church TV, RIP.ie, and the Irish Independent. As I was walking out the door, she asked would I show her how to write a condolence on RIP.ie—the site recording all Ireland's deaths—on my next visit. In Ireland, it's probably the only website more popular than Pornhub. The Irish still like to say a fond farewell to people on the move to the next world—a point in our favour as a nation. However, when I returned a few days later, she'd it figured out. I was impressed, I must admit.

'How did you do that?'

Then she gave me one of her smiles that indicated she'd executed one of her not-quite-straightforward logic experiments.

'I did a few practice ones.'

'How do you mean you did a few practice ones?'

This was met with the following flood of revelations.

'Sure, I went into County Dublin on RIP.ie and found a few people that passed away, God rest them. Then wrote them a short message and hit Submit—and sure the condolence message went through when I did that. I was getting stuck on Preview. You have to hit Submit—that's the key to it. You can't just preview, you have to hit Submit then as well. I did a few more just to be sure.'

'You've started writing shagging condolences to people you don't know?'

'Sure won't they be delighted in Dublin. They never had funerals like we had down the country—when you could have funerals, that is. I mean, there were only six messages on one of the people I did. Imagine—only six condolences! When you look up Galway, sure it's full of condolences, you know. And Mayo too—full of them.'

It brought to mind the scene from the Michael Collins movie where Liam Neeson reads a newspaper headline about his young Irish rebels who were out the previous 1920 evening, gunning down the British:

'Riddled with bullets, it says here, lads… riddled… we can't afford to be going around riddling people with bullets, lads. They don't grow on trees.'

My mother might need a dressing-down from the ghost of Michael Collins about riddling the countryside in condolences.

'So this book—what's it called?' she finally enquired again.

"The Real Anthony Fauci',' I replied.

'Who is he?'

I allowed myself a smile in advance.

'Well, I suppose he's a bit like Charlie Haughey—minus the great Leaving Cert results… we'll see if we can download it the next time I'm out, if you like.'

She seemed to like this idea. She's waking up a little, I thought to myself. Who knows—with a bit of luck she might figure out how to riddle Anthony Fauci with condolences before my next visit.

As I drove out the driveway that night, I looked across the road to the field of midnight feasts. It was at that moment the childhood memories started flooding back—seemingly spontaneous, unprompted, and unconnected. Now, as I sit here piecing it all together tonight, I can finally see a streak of moonlight.

When I woke up on a ditch, startled and unsure, she was the one who walked me back home. Someday, when I find my way and steady my feet, I'll need to do more in return.

Saoirse Creatives

In the first hour, the middle-aged lady spoke of her brother. Her love for him was clear and deep, as was the pain from the split between them now. Another house divided by a single decision. One after another people stood and plainly spoke—the raw emotion palpable. I observed the crowded room and absorbed my surroundings. It was a surprising start and energy—hurt, grief, some anger and explosions of relief combined.

I searched for the faces of my own clan—my son, brother, sister and father—all helping out for the day before I remembered I'd posted most of them to a location a mile away. A hundred tiny worries fought for the attention of my mind but were dispelled by this new energy flowing through the room. I could trust my own people, it seemed, to communicate.

Of course, I had the same difference of opinion with my family as the woman had with her brother, but fracture and conflict were old friends in the home of my younger self. Argument and raging emotion often erupted in those days, but, over time, a by-product was forged: a spirit for the white sheep and stray black ones to occasionally drink together from the same watering hole. I have come to believe there are many gifts in trauma, if you can just stay upright long enough to scavenge through the wreckage and unearth them. No easy task, I know.

The woman's words brought to mind a little jewel in my own relationship with parents and siblings. They'd want the best for me even when I'm standing on the opposite bank of the Rubicon from them. They'd give their best for me too. I wouldn't trust anyone else to try this adventure out with, on this weekend of weekends. I was grateful for my foul-weather family on this, the fairest of days. There would be rocky times ahead again no doubt but I recorded the new understanding and moved on.

As each voice rose to address the gathering, the vibration moved from wounds of the recent past to other things. Shortly after, I felt a fresh cologne in the air, a scent that everything would work out. Each new accent packaged new ideas, artistry, music and information from old, sometimes life-changing experiences. There was a thirst for the knowledge, it seemed, and still more voices to advise on what to do with it through practical husbandry. I drank coffee, leaned back against the wall, and reminded myself not to get in the way.

Much earlier, up at the community centre, I watched as the dawn sun blitzed the piercing, still cold, I remembered the words of the cliff guide:

'The weekend's promised sunny. Great weather for a walk along the cliffs.'

The first piece was falling into place, I thought, as his prophecy came true. I carried out a quick scan of the car park, playground, main hall, and vestibule of the second gathering site. Outside, you could gaze down on the Cliffs of Moher and the Atlantic Ocean. Inside, I marvelled at the projector, screen, mixing system, expensive speaker, microphones, and stands that manifested themselves out of thin air. I recalled the furrowed brow and argument with my brother about the scores of technical items I hadn't thought of the night before. I knew he'd be fine up here, figuring details out on the fly, and that important missing pieces would arrive. He was less than certain.

'You need to worry about these things,' he chided.

'You only need to worry about what I tell you to worry about,' I chipped back.

Thankfully, soon after this terse exchange, two musical elves appeared and banished the nervous tension with their smiles, laughter, and a bootful of sonic gifts. The same pair of elven creatures spent the weekend quietly sharing their wondrous talents on fiddle and bodhrán. Any time I caught a glimpse of these magical beings over the weekend, they were busy sprinkling faerie dust on good things—helping to make them great.

I left this place in the hands of my sister and brother—safe in the knowledge they wouldn't be the type to grumble about serving tea, coffee, and moving chairs around. Much later, when I had a spare moment to revisit this place, they spoke in wonder of the laughter lady's gifted performance, and the man talking about dimensions far removed from most earthly sensibilities.

'I mean, he's out there—he's really fucking out there, that fella.'

My brother relayed the last speaker's subject matter to my sister and me with hands spread high and wide above his head and eyes bulging wide to indicate the full extent of this human's out-there-ed-ness.

We laughed at his performative and theatrical rendition of these particular proceedings. We both agreed too that my brother bore more than a passing resemblance to the same man in both sunny disposition and easy comfort with strangers. Out-there-ed-ness might catch on.

And on it went. The first night built to an almost explosive crescendo of joyousness and release. At least it felt that way. A solo guitarist and one funny man did that. And, of course, the elves. At that stage they had impishly added to their number.

Later, as I dropped the old man home, I wondered what he had made of the funny man.

'Ah brilliant, just brilliant—never enjoyed a weekend as much as this.'

There might be hope for this world yet, I thought, as he half-dozed off in the passenger seat. I dropped him off and sat in the car a while alone—too juiced for sleep and too afraid to examine deeply the day just past for fear of damaging the one that lay ahead. So, instead, I smoked and drank in some music from the radio.

I thought briefly of the pension-aged gentleman who came alone to the proceedings and shook my hand and thanked me before the evening's festivities began—his grip, calloused skin, and the power of hands that intimately knew a life of manual labour. He was first to arrive both evening and morning. He hardly missed a voice all weekend, and I quietly admonished myself for not spending more time chatting with him and for not introducing him to my father.

The highs of the night were replaced by a gentle and meditative descent on the Sunday that followed. The younger man and older woman brought tears with beautiful poetry and music—a spiritual reminder of things that had happened and of people who had sadly passed on to the next world. I removed myself for a few moments and shed salty tears of sorrow and quiet joy. An older man reminded the gathering of the history of this land that we stood on—and who we were as a people and ought to consider being again. The power of those middle hours was undeniable.

Meanwhile, my talented cousin and a gorgeous Portuguese couple entertained the little people with art and vibrant colour. Of course, schedules ran long and certain plans never materialised, but the powerful, growing energy seemed intent on steamrolling any big problems out of its path. I was mightily glad of the assistance. There was more—much more—over the two days. These are just some snippets that have jumped into my consciousness right now, pleasurably recorded here for posterity.

At the end I retreated to the aunt's place for some food and waited for those hardy cliff-walkers to return. The yoga woman relayed that the views were spectacular on such a fine day and that the path and pace chosen by the guide were appreciated by all—as was his knowledge and good humour.

Before she left, she lowered her voice and placed the final jigsaw piece of the weekend down on the table.

'At the bottom, I looked back up to the cliffs one last time, and I noticed some clouds starting to form... now isn't that interesting... first time I've seen any clouds since we got here.'

I nodded in agreement. Interesting indeed—but I wasn't sure what, if anything, to make of it. Perhaps Saoirse's work was done for now on this stretch of rock—busy as she is with many more places to go and black sheep to attend.

Glad she stuck around as long as she did.

Interlude: Primroses

Sometimes I write just for the pure pleasure of it, a breath-out pause. I'm going to try and say more with a little less tonight. Unfortunately, this makes my job harder, not easier. My own reading capacity and attention span have diminished in recent years—which means much of yours is probably totally fucked too. No offence. The obvious culprit: digitally infiltrated, defenceless minds. If you're the exception to the rule—my heartiest congratulations.

I'm house-sitting and a beautiful evening is chugging to a close here in the shadow of some Burren hills. I sit at a small kitchen table gazing out at a wild, overgrown front garden teeming with life. Each passing April day stretches an extended hand towards summer. The half-light each evening stretches further and further into the cosmic distance. The fading light and near-cloudless skyline the perfect canvas for the night to, perhaps, brush in a curved moon and a star or two. Or many. The possibilities seem endless—and mostly good.

The heavens are at peace for a small while.

Earlier, on a lazy smoke break—one filled with loud, busy thoughts—a noise filled the air, distracting me from my distracting mind conversations. The backing vocals were invisible birds, chirping deliriously somewhere beyond the old stone boundary wall. Noticing their singing helped settle my thoughts down. Like trusty tour guides, they pointed to the simple wonders all around.

Once upon a time, I knew the names of all the birds and all of the trees and all of the flowers whenever I happened upon them on my childhood travels through dirty ditches and bramble bushes.

But now I could fill a library with all of the natural intelligence I've casually forgotten.

'All life is here, all life is here,' the birds seemed to chorus in a certain unison.

Back in the present, another revelation arrives as I listen to nature's symphony gently begin to wind down into the silence of the slow-approaching night. Outside, I glance through the kitchen window at the table inside and observe my laptop and smartphones (yes, phones, plural).

What's in this triumvirate of devilry, I wonder? The fresh breeze fills my lungs with a type of oxygen that indicates I may not have pondered this question in this particular fashion before. From this observation post—just outside the glass pane—it seems to me the answer is: not much and far too much.

Anxiety, distraction, negativity, and the whole goddamn world at my fingertips.

'Life isn't in there, life isn't in there,' the now-sleeping birds might caw. Increasingly, answers aren't in there either. Artificial intelligence is in there, though—no doubt unimpressed that I'm outside by the garden and not at the table, I suspect. I turn away from the window and absorb the quiet peace of the outside world again. Lying back against the windowsill, I notice the primroses for the first time—growing in clumps near the entrance gatepost. A memory triggers from my childhood.

Back then, as the evenings stretched, the amount of time spent outdoors—wandering through fields, climbing ash trees, breaking into hay barns, and gifting neighbours with half-built treehouses—expanded too. My friend and I would be unearthed not by the beep of a phone but usually by the worried shouts of my mother vibrating into earshot—announcing a dinner growing cold. Her calls would snap me out of my nature trance, beckoning in the sounds of trouble on the wind and starvation in my stomach. Sometimes, though, on perfect nights like this one, these exhilarating explorations could go on till the arrival of the moon and the stars.

Life seemed everywhere outside my kitchen window then. A universe ever-expanding and yet profoundly understandable and simple—when a sheepish smile and a muddied fist of primroses solved a lot of my day-to-day mischief-making and hunger problems. There are nights when the buzz-buzz of my phone and racing thoughts won't let me rest—when sleep comes dropping slow. Tonight, though, the sky is at peace and the garden is pocketed with primroses. The beauty and mystery of both consume me with stillness.

How could anyone possibly sleep on a night like this one?

PART 2: BRIGID

A Decision and a Little News

'And near me on the grass lies Glanvill's book—Come, let me read the oft-read tale again! The story of the Oxford scholar poor, Of pregnant parts and quick inventive brain, Who, tired of knocking at preferment's door, One summer-morn forsook His friends, and went to learn the gipsy-lore, And roam'd the world with that wild brotherhood, And came, as most men deem'd, to little good, But came to Oxford and his friends no more.'

— Extract from 'The Scholar Gipsy', by Matthew Arnold.

It's been a while since I've sat to write a personal reflection. I won't keep you long, but I suppose there is news to get off my chest. I should know, at this age of my life, that avoiding necessary reflection and action paralyses me slowly from the head down. Usually, reflection requires a level of introspection on something that I'm uncomfortable addressing in the moment. This is the primary reason I've managed to waste quite a considerable amount of my life. Indecision or procrastination stymies growth—I know this. Yet, I don't know it too. Sometimes, I guess, you need to be a bit of a cunt with yourself to get things moving along.

For most of the pandemic, I was in a work position that allowed me to carry out my functions from home. It was a blessing insofar as it afforded me the opportunity to write about the tyranny of the times without the outside world interfering with my thought processes too much. While, for many, the years 2020 and 2021 will be remembered as some of the darkest in living memory, for me they were among the best periods of my life. I found a freedom in the jail cell of pandemic restrictions that I would never have unearthed without it. Battered by two years of ugly scientific words, I slowly comprehended something: only the swords of inner poetry could defeat them. A key to my writing in this period was the liberation I found within—a discovery that came courtesy of the luxury of working my 'real job' from the kitchen table.

All good things come to an end, though. I held out for as long as I could, but since early spring I've been back on the commuter's trail. The kitchen table traded in for the office chair. After a week back in the saddle and two-hour daily round trips to my workplace, I knew, deep down, that it was time to leave this world behind me. However, I struggled to turn the key marked 'radical change' in the ignition switch. Executing the decision was more difficult than I had anticipated, and taking a leap into the unknown was not as easy as I might first have imagined. After twenty-five years as part of the Irish workforce, I've never quit a job without having another one already lined up to take its place.

Until now.

Two Mondays ago, I landed down at work and into the office, sat down at my desk, and flipped open the laptop. Before I knew it, I had typed out my resignation letter. Then took a sip of my stale canteen coffee and hit send with a little extra juice. Short and sweet. I looked around at the bent heads peering into their digital screens and settling into their workday. I was still in their midst but no longer one of their number. Funny thing—I didn't wake up that morning and plan to do it. It was as if my other self, this demon and sometime angel that sits on my shoulder, tired of my dithering, elbowed me aside.

Tappity-tap, tappity-tap—and in seconds, my life as an unremarkable participant in Ireland's technology industry had drawn to a close. The relief was instant and almost overwhelming. I needed to escape the fluorescent lighting to gather my thoughts, so I nipped out to the car park and sat into my car. I lit a cigarette and could feel the tears welling up inside, my right hand shaking slightly as I drew a drag and inhaled the smoke. Relief and fear began running down the sides of my cheeks. I could see a security guard chatting with a couple of visitors filling out forms and looking to gain entry to the factory at the entrance hut. I'd be forgotten soon enough.

The voice in my head—the expert typer of resignation letters—wasn't too teary-eyed; he asked a question and issued an instruction.

'How much more of your fucking life are you gonna waste? Start the car and get the fuck out of this place.'

Pertinent question—and, for once, I did as I was instructed to do. So, I eased out the electronic security gates and headed for Tuam. Driving out of one world and into quite another.

A Rendezvous with Aloneness

Finally, my aloneness could be rejected no longer. Like an old hang-dog friend, intimate with the patterns of my life yet much under-appreciated. And knowing this, he sensed exactly where to sit and where to position himself for my imminent arrival.

Our rendezvous was on Lahinch strand, a stretch of perfect sand on the west coast—no surprise on location, for this was a week made for such places. The tourist village normally heaves with humanity during the summer's sweet spot, all in search of fun and some sun-kissed fantasticness.

It was the best of weeks and the worst of weeks for me. Truly. But I knew a clock was ticking somewhere, and I could avoid this particular appointment no longer. So, I didn't.

Early Saturday, some necessarily deep words were exchanged. They hurt the two of us. All that remained was to visit my old friend and mark the occasion in silence. I grabbed a towel, a new book, cigarettes, and sat into the car and drove.

At journey's end, I found myself outside Lahinch golf club, the coastal hotspot mobbed with youth, white teeth and fancy Dublin car registration plates. The promenade was packed; the Atlantic tide had just come fully in and the beach was nowhere to be seen. I would have to wait a while.

I sat in the car, charged my phone, and waited as patiently as I could for the tide to ebb out. It would take hours for the waters to recede from the rocks and for the slicks of wet sand to reveal themselves—but I knew he'd be down there somewhere when they did.

I began to read *A Zealous Priest*, a book about the murder of Galway priest Fr. Michael Griffin in 1920. I was struck by the incidental references to the Irish Parliamentary Party—the old 'Home Rule' party—and John Redmond. How quickly fortunes can change, I thought. In 1914 the Irish Parliamentary Party were the dominant political force in Ireland.

By 1918?

Obliterated by Sinn Féin—and Redmond was dead. The thought gave me a brief shiver, but a little hope too. You never know when things will suddenly collapse—or conversely, come unexpectedly together.

That's life really, isn't it?

Slow-slow-slow—quick-quick-quick-slow—and then possibly dead.

I went to start the engine for a quick spin up to Liscannor village and discovered my battery was dead. I decided I'd rather stub cigarette butts out on my eyeballs than introduce my red-and-black jump leads into a conversation with this bank holiday crowd. Which was probably unfair of me.

Besides, I had a towel, a book, twenty-odd cigarettes, and, after the previous weekend, a developing fondness for sleeping in my car. If I could just negotiate all the shiny teeth I might get out of this thing alive, I figured.

Down a car and with no beach in sight, I stretched my legs along the short promenade and thought of something someone had mentioned in passing on Substack recently.

Alcoholics Anonymous was the place where I too first began to consider, in earnest, a power higher than my own ego—my first conscious realisation of the might of energy and raw emotion. I've often thought, since those early encounters, that raw emotional honesty obliterates all lies. As if the truth is pulled from your very being by the nobility of a flawed man or woman laying bare their most embarrassing and damaging traits.

How else could one respond to such majesty?

Thinking of AA reminded me of an encounter, during my dreamlike midweek wanderings around Connemara, with three bar staff in Leenane. I was ordering food, a pint of Guinness, and a Heineken Zero.

All three staff were mainland European, as far as I could tell. When I asked for the Guinness, the young chap said he wasn't sure the hotel had any. Then he gingerly picked up a pint glass and tried the Guinness tap for size. Satisfied that liquid was pouring out, he filled the glass and plopped it on the counter in front of me without allowing it time to settle. He looked at the glass, and I looked at him.

'I don't think it's working,' he said, or words to that effect.

The other two looked none the wiser as to why the pint was temporarily brown and not black. I half-hoped a matronly mountain woman from the 1950s might appear with a slash-hook and mistake the trio for a field of dense thistles.

I was on a radio show last week, and the host asked me what constitutes Irish culture.

Well, how long is a piece of string?

Guinness is part of our culture—and believe me, no one knows the good, the bad, and the ugly of it better than I do. Are we consigning the memory of Guinness to history too? Perhaps Guinness is racist—after all, why should a creamy head be allowed to sit atop all that dark stout goodness?

Joking aside, I remember well the panic that would erupt if, in any pub I worked in, we were down to our last barrel a day before the delivery. Pubs would cadge barrels from one another to avoid the mortal embarrassment of running out of Guinness. To my knowledge it never, ever happened. Never mind not knowing how to pour a pint and let it settle. And not cringing.

Eventually, the tide edged out into the bay just enough to let me shuffle down the steps and land on a patch of beach. It was late evening; the sun was sinking, shadows lengthening. The crowds had thinned, and only a dozen or so people chanced a swim at this far remove from the heat of the day.

My mind began to quiet, and my eyes followed the sunset dancing across the still waters.

'You're alone again, I see… you're truly feeling it this time,' he said as he enveloped me completely.

'I am,' said I.

'How do you feel then?'

'Insignificant.'

'Good, good,' he smiled sadly. 'You might be ready for someone else soon.'

We walked up the steps together and soon after sat into the car in silence. I turned the key—the engine started first time. I looked over to him in amazement, but he was gone from the passenger seat. I nodded slowly to myself, then stuck the car into reverse and began to back out. A beautiful Strawberry Moon rose in my rear-view mirror. I eased onto the road, my aloneness in peaceful retreat. Soon, the night blanketed me—and I hoped dreams might return once more.

Brigid

So, there I was sitting back in my new old car outside a petrol station in Castlebar. I was two hours into what I only understood later on to be my first proper adventure with Brigid. Munching away on a Corrib Oil salad bowl. I was absolutely livid with myself. My anger, I should add, had little to do with the contents of my nutritious salad, which, in fairness, contained all of my preferred vegetables: namely, boiled eggs and freshly picked mayonnaise from the organic Hellmann's farm three miles down the road.

No, my raging internal ire was directed at something else entirely, a self-inflicted wound I'd created out of thin air due to my chronic inattentiveness and casual nature. As I quickly muttered through the full suite of four-letter words in my vocabulary box, I glanced up from my bowl. The vista that greeted me through the windscreen of my blue Peugeot blackened my mood even further. Two members of the Garda Síochána, the Irish police force in new money, were exiting their jeep and approaching my vehicle with intent. A man and a woman. Ah, wonderful, just fucking wonderful, I thought.

One immediate problem had now turned into two.

As I rolled down my window, the female Garda got straight down to business and asked to see my driver's licence. I enquired politely as to why anyone in the wide, earthly world would want to see that pesky old thing. I privately cursed myself for not knowing enough about the law and my rights in this situation.

'You're not displaying valid car tax or an insurance disc,' she observed while handing my driver's licence over to the male Garda for closer inspection. Her assured method of delivery was somewhere between a question and a statement of fact. I concluded by her actions and confidence that she was probably both the beauty and brains of this operation. So, I focused my gaze on her and reserved zero attention for her male colleague examining my photo ID. A strategy, I deduced, that allowed ample time for the female officer to go right ahead and fall fully in love with me.

Problematically, however, I think she was expecting a response to her question-cum-statement which was another stumbling block to add to the mounting pile on the dashboard. Inconveniently, the sum total of people who fall in love with me after I open my mouth might well be close to zero or perhaps even a negative number.

As I formulated a reply, I was momentarily reminded of the Saoirse gathering in Doolin eighteen months earlier with the group of like-minded insurance disc dodgers. Late on the Sunday afternoon, an attractive young woman was giving a very fine and knowledgeable presentation on cryptocurrency and the importance of decentralised networks. At the end, a member of the audience asked her a question:

'What are the income tax implications of what you are talking about?'

'Oh well, that depends,' she replied.

'Depends on what?'

'It depends on whether you believe in the concept of income tax or not.'

Fortunately or unfortunately, I somewhat believe in the concept of motor insurance. For my car was actually insured, and so I decided to elaborate a little on the situation.

'It's insured, but I don't have the disc yet—I'm only after purchasing the car last weekend.'

The male Garda jumped in at this point and asked where I was from. I was thinking of getting annoyed and not telling him, but then the notion struck me to do the exact opposite.

'I'm from Tuam and I'm heading up into the Nephin mountains to a natural spring to fill up on water, but I've got a problem.'

I had a boot full of empty one-litre glass bottles and a five-litre plastic drum. Warming to the glasnost theme, I was now dying to be asked all about the off-grid shenanigans I had planned for the afternoon. However, the female Garda interrupted my thought flow and said something peculiar. She smiled and handed me back my licence, which the male Garda had just handed back to her.

'It's OK, we know it's insured.'

Only later did I note the oddness of this line and wonder how they knew, but, in the moment, ploughed on past what she said to discuss my other problem with her. I did this as a form of distraction and also because it seemed we were at the very least fast-tracking to be lifelong friends and quite possibly future lovers. As I sit here typing, another thing only dawns on me now. If my first problem hadn't happened, then the arrival of the second—the police issue—would never have materialised as I'd have already exited the Corrib Oil before their appearance on the forecourt.

'You know the reason I'm sitting here is because I'm after putting about €25 of petrol into my car's diesel tank.'

Well, I might as well have stated I had explosives strapped to my chest—so fast did the dynamic duo scarper away from my old jalopy. So, I guess if quick escape from the clutches of the Garda Síochána is ever a future goal, I'll just present them with a problem I need help with and watch them fade away into the distance.

So, with one problem successfully negotiated, I returned to my original sin and salad. I rang three separate garages in Castlebar and, curiously, all three returned the same answer to my pleas for help.

'I'm away on holidays this week.'

Fuckity fuck fuck fuck.

In desperation, I began Googling 'What to do when an idiot-like creature pumps petrol into your diesel tank'.

Eventually, I happened upon one website that advised that it might not be the end of the world. In fact, the text read that as long as 95% of the fuel in the tank was diesel, the car would probably be fine. So, my Peugeot 306's 60-litre diesel tank had room for a maximum of 3 litres of petrol. Frustratingly, I'd just blasted between 13 and 14 litres of petrol into the car. Hmmm, not good.

After a quick calculation, I figured that if I filled the rest of the tank with diesel it would bring me to just over 75% diesel. Perhaps 95% was a mere amber warning signal but not quite burning in hell territory. Remember, I just bought this car, with a helping loan from a soul-friend. So this wasn't a risk I could afford to take. The next step was obvious. Call another garage and empty the tank.

Isn't that right?

Well, this unfortunately brings us to a fundamental short-circuit problem throughout the existence of me. Obviously, what happened next was I filled the tank up to the brim, this time with the correct fuel, and started the engine. It let out a little raspy cough to clear her throat, then purred to life. Then, I pointed the 76% diesel-fuelled car in the general direction of Westport and took my chances.

I recited a decade of the rosary as I drove and began to think. I remembered back to the Sunday evening just past and a walk down a tree-lined byroad possessing possible faerie vibes. It was late evening but still bright when I parked up the car on a little lay-by on the laneway. The lay-by had a kind of monument dedicated to someone who had passed tragically away, as I recall, with flowers and a jug of holy water. For some reason I grabbed the jug and flicked some holy water onto my new car with a sign of the cross.

Earlier, and on the day before, when I flicked down the sun visor in the car, I noticed a little Padre Pio holy pin was fastened to it on the inside. I was most happy to see it there for some reason. I place significance on these types of things now in a manner I never did before. I accept they are significant without the requirement of any type of proof. The key for me is just to pay attention and accept. So, I hoped and prayed that my attention to these two tiny things—Padre Pio and the holy water—might outweigh my inattention and risk-taking at the petrol station. As crazy as that undoubtedly sounds.

The new Castlebar–Westport motorway also allows for the bypass of Westport town and, as I was headed for Newport, I took it. The bypass brought me very close to the big pharmaceutical multinational in the town where I once had worked and which marked my last full-time job in the old world. I felt relieved to be on the far side of their electronic barriers and on the road to Nephin.

Miraculously, thirty minutes later I was filling up on water and not petrol from the roadside mountain spring a few miles past the village of Furnace and across the road from a lake basking in sunshine. The car was purring like she might be ready for a season of Formula One racing. I completed my water mission and filled up the last bottle. I drank it down, pausing for a moment to drink in some of the stunning scenery too.

I decided to keep travelling further up and closer to the National Park. Not long after I stumbled upon a house of prayer, one I'd come upon before—Shramore Church. A prefab structure but picturesque too. Two elderly men and a woman were outside chatting. One of the men had one of those old yellow weed-killer containers on his back for spraying weeds. Totally illegal down in the bustling streets of Westport no doubt but rather apt for the mountains and slaying spiritual demons, I thought to myself.

I said a brief hello, wandered into the church, lit a couple of candles, and said another decade of the rosary. I took a few photographs of the interior as it was quite beautiful in a simple way. The windows were tiny, almost like square portholes. Some with clear glass and some stained in bright, vibrant colours. One was dedicated to St. Bridget and one to Our Lady and another to St. Columcille. This sparked an idea in my head as I left the church. On exit, I was happy to note the keeper of the chapel didn't immediately feel the need to shower me with a blast of weed-killer.

The newly christened Brigid and I made our way slowly back down the mountain and soon arrived back into Newport. I pulled into a petrol station and decided the best course of action might be to ram another few litres of diesel into the car. I managed to get another five into the tank and walked into the shop and immediately became engaged in a staring competition with the coffee machine. I hit the black Americano button instead of latte and decided that while I didn't lose the eyeballing contest, I didn't win it either. A score draw.

So, I took my black coffee out to Brigid and half-heartedly tried to calculate how close her diesel tank was to the 95% mark. I was less worried than before and it probably had something to do with my car completing the Padre Pio—holy water—Brigid trinity.

I suppose, though, as I sit here thinking about the whole escapade now—something strikes me. Perhaps, in the end, it's not all about whether we hit perfection or the 95% mark when we move on to whatever awaits us in the next world. But how much I've added to my spiritual tank or helped others to fill theirs. Have I learned or am I correctly learning my individual method of processing my shadow into some form of light?

Allowing too much petrol into the diesel tank will destroy the car. But don't each and every one of us start on the road with a little petrol dirtying our diesel?

Isn't that the journey?

We all start with some darkness and some light. And maybe that is the lesson. I need to pay more attention to what I allow into my tank, for it's how we process the dirty petrol that determines how long it takes to arrive at the sunny mountain spring.

What Mike Tyson taught me about Spirituality

Any time I muse on matters of the spirit—or even Himself—some readers on Substack get a little wobbly. But all I'm really talking about is a belief in something—or someone—much greater than myself. That's it. I'm not promoting my concept of what this particular someone or something might be; I'm inviting the reader to contemplate what it might mean to them—or not.

And boy, did I need a little help from Himself today. Quite frequently, when a negative mood or emotion strikes, it can leave me in a funk of anger bordering on rage for a few days, or occasionally even longer. I am determined enough that this carry-on might fade away into the future with a little work. Microscopic resentments can suddenly start moving mountains.

So, this morning, instead of wallowing in gloom, I revved up Brigid and pointed her in the general direction of a church I know—a city chapel where I usually find some peace. However, a negative thought struck me as I hit the motorway: the fucking laptop.

My typing machine has been stranded in the Midlands since I attended an event there ten days ago, and I had made plans with the kindly owner of the property to collect it this afternoon. The last few articles I've written have been compiled on a notebook with three keys missing, and tapping these out has been a monstrous pain in the hole.

'What to do… what to do…,' I wondered.

Recently, during the witching hours before dawn, I came across a video interview with Mike Tyson. I listened to the first couple of minutes and immediately understood his words had significance for me, but I was half-asleep and parked it for future consumption. Now, Tyson—for the unfamiliar—is the former undisputed heavyweight boxing champion of the world, but more than that, in my opinion, is also one of the most interesting spiritual characters currently alive. Yes, you read that last line correctly. Allow me to make the case.

Any close followers of his life path will know he's been on his own spirit quest searching for light and peace over the last number of years. But my interest in him is centred on his darkness. His epic struggle with the shadows inside is fascinating to observe as they frequently still manifest in the outer world. Increasingly, I find myself trying to learn from his lessons.

Why, though?

Good question.

Tyson's worst demons seem to be as close to pitch black as it is possible to find in a human. It is frankly amazing that a figure so well-known is so willing to talk about them openly and publicly. Conversely, it also seems to me that when his lightness shines it is almost blinding in its brilliance. I struggle to accept aspects of my own shadow exist, never mind contemplating the application of a forensic eye on them. Listening to someone darker go deeper helps. So today, as I drove off in search of some peace, I flicked on the Tyson clip I'd discovered a few nights previously and began to listen.

'I had to be beaten into submission. It didn't happen overnight; I had to go to prison for this. I had to lose all my money for this. I had to lose my wife; I had to lose my gold-digger girlfriends, whom I loved so much. I had to lose all that stuff for this—to get whatever I have, whatever you think I have. It's all about loss. It ain't all about gains. My gains are all about loss.' —Mike Tyson

What is the 'this' he was referring to? I wondered and began chewing on it. Perhaps the spiritual path, and the droplets of peace that sometimes—unexpectedly—settle onto the road in front of your feet, offering encouragement to keep shuffling along. A temporary reprieve from the shadow that lurks, ever present, in the background. In one sense I've materially lost a lot over the last eighteen months and the ever-present questions in my head are:

Are these signs of progress or regression?

Am I inching towards the 'This' that Tyson speaks of?

Soon, a decision was required. I was approaching the exit of the M17. Edge right for Galway and a church, or veer left for Dublin and the Midlands. 'Fuck it,' I thought. The gospel of Mike Tyson would have to do—I needed the shagging laptop back. Brigid indicated left while I refocused on the conversation at play in my ears. In it, Tyson was giving advice to a very talented fighter. Again, shards of bright and hard-won wisdom whispered through my earbuds and shone in through the windscreen.

'One thing I'm gonna tell you—and this is spiritual, right. See all your fights and stuff? All your knockouts—it's spectacular.

You know what that means?

All this good stuff that is happening to you—do you know what that means? It means you're favoured by God.

You know that, right?'

A brief pause followed before he returned to deliver the knockout punch.

'But when you're favoured by God, you're also favoured by the devil. He's coming for you too. So you've gotta be strong and stay on the right side. Whose side are you going to go on? He's going to give you power too. He's gonna get in your head too. But whose side are you gonna stay with? You stay with who brought you here. You go home with the guy who brought you to the dance. God loves you, but so does he. He's after you too. It's a war.' —Mike Tyson

I don't think I've ever heard something so profoundly true for me in my whole life. When an inner light falteringly begins to shine—or flickers on—the first fucker to notice is my inner darkness, and that guy sure as hell does not appreciate too much illumination. Teeth come out, bared. Listening to this segment, I was struck by a truth: the struggle will be always. There is no end. Somewhere after the toll bridge in Loughrea I managed to get past the sadness of this new, thudding realisation; I felt a little better—but not much.

The road is hard, but 'this' is the correct road for me—that's all I can muster at the moment. It might be a lonely road. I might fuck it up from time to time. It might seem a crazy path, and it might seem sparsely populated, but such is the path I've chosen, and that is the price that needs to be paid. I'm either going to stop doubting this notion in future or have to turn the car around.

Even at its worst, life is worth living, and even at my worst I've never wished I were not living. In fact, in those darker and more fearful moments, the sanctity of life has often resonated at its strongest. A little sun broke through the clouds at this thought, metaphorically and literally, as I approached my destination.

Hmmm, maybe I had taken the correct exit off the motorway after all.

Soon, I was chatting with the owner, and I safely retrieved my laptop. As we parted, he offered an invitation:

'We're having Mass and Benediction here tomorrow evening; I'm expecting a good crowd. There's a BBQ as well—would you like to come along?'

I couldn't quite believe the offer and its welcome timing. I nodded my head, mumbled a yes, and said a quick goodbye before the damn gratefulness started pouring out of my eye sockets.

Mike Tyson and Himself had shown up on the same exit of the motorway.

The Remnant

remnant

noun

A part or quantity that is left after the greater part has been used, removed, or destroyed.

I looked around at the assorted bunch of heads and bodies squeezed and tightly packed into the room. One hundred, maybe one hundred and fifty, I guesstimated.

The word 'remnant' sprang from my senses.

A remnant of Irish faith but, oddly, a huddle of spirits searching for more—and not less—from their church. This wasn't a spoken utterance from the crowd but something I kind of felt floating in the air, rightly or wrongly. A refreshing energy scented the place. It seemed both ancient and yet modern too. I scanned the room for a place to sit and I locked onto a couple of empty chairs near the back wall.

Our shoulders rubbed as I sat down in the last row of this home chapel. Her hair was brown and rainy-wet and her teenage daughter's eyes were blue and sparkling with life. The seats were tightly squished together to accommodate the crowd, a crowd now threatening to spill into the adjoining courtyard. Our shoulders mashed together once more as another woman sat down to my left in the last remaining chair. I edged my seat to the right a little to give the new arrival some breathing space. I glanced across to the brown-haired woman to apologise but she beat me to the punch.

'Sorry, me shoulders are damp, we've been walking all day and me and my daughter are soaked through. I hope I don't get you too wet.'

I wasn't bothered one way or the other. Her cheeks still glowed a rosy red from her outdoor adventures in the elements and I was rather interested to learn why she was trudging all day in the wind and autumnal rain.

'Why were you out walking all day?' I enquired.

'Well, we've been walking for two days carrying the cross,' she answered happily.

'The cross?' I said dumbly.

'Yes, our Lord Jesus on the cross. Thirty-three miles we've walked, me and me daughter. Our group started in Roscommon yesterday and then walked here from Ballinasloe this morning.'

Interesting, I thought. Very interesting indeed. We fell into a short whispered conversation and I soon learned there were four different groups from Ireland's four provinces out gallivanting in the jumbled-up Irish wind, rain and sunshine. All had walked exactly thirty-three miles from four different starting points, depending on their province, and they all converged on Clonmacnoise that evening.

Clonmacnoise, I should note, was founded by St Ciarán in the 6th century on the banks of the River Shannon. It stands as one of Ireland's most sacred monastic sites, if not the most sacred. Historically, it's a place where contemplation, scholarship, and spirituality have intertwined down through the Irish ages. Possessed of round towers, stone crosses, the ruins of monks' dwelling places and ancient graves, it's a parcel of spiritual land I try to visit often and I was glad to discover on this visit a Catholic crew whose vibe matched my own.

As the brown-haired woman filled me in on her walk to Clonmacnoise, I was struck again by how radiant and alive her daughter appeared as she listened to her mother recount their experiences of the previous forty-eight hours. This was a kid who wanted to be at this Mass with her mother. Most unusual and heart-warming.

Before long a hush descended and cut short our chatter as a serious-looking priest at the top of the room threw a few shapes to begin proceedings. I looked across the gathering and could see a German Shepherd-looking dog stretched out on a couch asleep. A husband and wife sat on the edge of the same settee, or near it, but were too polite to disturb the dog or try to move him to make a bit more room for themselves.

In my memory, which I must admit can be quite shaky on recall, it seemed there was a sermon at the beginning and in the middle of the Mass too. At some point the Ten Commandments and purgatory were introduced into the priestly conversation with the congregation. I closed my eyes and kept them closed for a good while. Read into that what you will, I suppose. I sometimes wonder if I am already settled into purgatory and perhaps even getting comfortable here. The priest rattled through the importance of adhering to the Ten Commandments, like a surgeon showing a class of medical students how to remove a cancer—one growth at a time.

Helpfully, though, the dog on the couch began to snore, which brought a low murmur of muffled laughter from the back of the room that lightened the seriousness of the subject matter. My higher power definitely has a sense of humour, is all I'll say.

One thing I've noticed since I began this cautious journey back into the formal structures of the church is that the earthly instruments of God or Jesus get in the way of my connection to Himself more often than they don't. I can be distracted easily. For example, if the Ten Commandments were a subject on the Leaving Certificate, I'd be constantly hovering around a Grade D and inherently know an A+ grade was most unlikely at any time in the future.

Don't get me wrong, it's very much no harm to get these reminders now and again and to feel bad about them and work on them, but many are already feeling bad enough. Too bad, probably. So, a little too much imbalance exists between a focus on sin and a focus on love for me.

I've come around, more and more, to the idea that I have to love my way out of my problems, which is an admission a middle-aged man wouldn't want to be saying out loud, in the cold light of day, too often in public. But even that goal is more of an obstacle than it might sound on first hearing, especially when I find it easier to hate than to love, and to criticise more than to praise. However, if you're pulsing out love, you're also beating back the darkness—or so runs my theory. To be frank, though, I'm not even sure how I might do this consistently without getting arrested or having Ballinasloe Mental Hospital reopened. At any rate, I'd better cease blathering about love, and all things nice, in case the Minister for the Environment hears about it and slaps a carbon tax down on top of the lot of us.

The prayers of the faithful were a most interesting affair. All the devotions were randomly offered up from people seated in the pews. These offerings went on for a good fifteen minutes and indicated to me that the place was jam-packed with like-minded people. Awesome, I thought. Faith-based new radicals. Normal people, in old parlance. Yet another new jigsaw piece—hitherto unknown—to add to the Irish resistance puzzle.

Now, based on the accents on display during this section of the Mass, it seemed to me that northerners made up more than one quarter of the audience. That is to say—Ulster was punching above its weight at this gathering.

A delicious thought hit my mind. Wouldn't there be a certain Irish irony and symmetry if it were northern devotion that saved the Irish faithful? If it was the light of their devotion—this remnant—surgically separated at the dawn of our independence, that came down to save the island from ever-expanding, never-ending globalism. And that isn't a strictly Catholic observation. I've noticed on my few trips across the border in the last two years that people of both strong Catholic and Protestant faith were in agreement on many of the hot-topic narratives running rampant across our shared island.

One young woman offered up prayers for the unborn—again, a northern voice. I noted the average age of the four provinces in attendance was probably lowest in this Ulster cohort. I remembered she was a member of a crew of maybe six or eight younger people that I observed earlier at the barbecue. All looked in their early thirties. The men were handsome, strong and fit, and as a Donegal man might put it, the women were wild beautiful.

The prayers went on and I found great comfort in listening to the different voices and mulling over the various concerns highlighted through prayer. Near the end, a woman offered up prayers for our leaders. I opened an eye and looked hopefully across to my German friend palmed out on the couch, half-hoping for a wise, canine bark of protest or two. He let me down, though, and snoozed on through it unperturbed. Afterwards, on calmer reflection, I grudgingly saw the wisdom of his quietness and conceded that clattering a couple of 'Our Fathers' down on top of their collective political heads mightn't automatically place me in the category of controlled opposition. Indeed, as I write, I'm slightly embarrassed at the impulse to exclude them from the prayers, as they need them more than most, I suspect.

After maybe eighty or ninety minutes, the Mass ended, but wondrously the time flew by. The din of the crowd rose and conversation bubbles began to break out all over this little home-shrine to faith. I took my leave at this point as I hadn't earned the right to walk and mingle amongst their number. Pausing only briefly, outside, to cup my hands and light a cigarette.

The autumnal darkness had fully descended and I was reminded for the first time this year that another season of long summer days was drawing to a close. How many seasons had I left? I idly pondered for a moment. I sat into Brigid and continued smoking peacefully enough, then looked out a final time at the lights of the house and chapel within and the people leaking out into the courtyard. Something was right about this place and the people who'd walked the thirty-three miles to arrive in it. That's all I can say really. Sitting and standing as they were, rubbing against the walls of the old monastic setting in Clonmacnoise and set against the backdrop of those ancient teachings and settlements of St Ciarán.

I was clueless as to what exactly was right about the whole experience. Yet, these new waves of emotion, recent additions to my life, started rumbling in the depths of me once more and I knew it was so. A stirring was upon me and I resigned myself to the cursed fact that ignoring it wouldn't work anymore. So, I dumped the fag into an empty coffee cup, stuck in the earbuds and decided not to avoid the inevitable. A song sprang to life, Brigid's engine purred and off we went—leaving behind an old site with new faces determined to carry their crosses and perhaps some of the crosses of this country too.

The remnant.

Again, the word pleased me, and I began to lose myself in the music of the night, in the rhythm of their might.

A Valley of Darkness

Write.

Just try to fucking write something down.

Anything.

Just tip-tap, or tap-tip

Or whatever the fuck.

Any words will do.

Words are oxygen.

But the oxygen tank is empty.

It was a cold, wet night and close to 2 am, when my friend and host for the evening opened the tall entrance gates to allow my exit. I slowed and rolled down my window to say a final goodbye and thank you. We had talked earlier, and he advised once more that I was in the valley and not to force anything. It was good advice and a fair summation of my predicament. I was down there for sure—surrounded by dense trees and thick timber and doubt and poisoned darts of blackness. I wasn't certain how I'd fallen into the valley this time, though. Which is a worry, moving forward. If I move forward, that is.

Wasn't the sun massaging its warmth down on top of my head a mere five minutes ago?

Or so it seems. The shadows are sapping more energy than on previous visits to the valley. My friend advised that there's something to be learned down here, but I'm in the mood for forgetfulness, not fucking lessons.

As I pulled gently away from the gates and the small gathering, my attention was mesmerised for a few seconds by some raindrops illuminated by Brigid's headlights. She'd been quiet lately—or maybe I'd been silently taking her for granted again. Anyway, the rain fell at angles somewhere between horizontal and vertical—silvery and softly translucent, but not quite oven-baked teardrops.

Yet.

Tender, slanty droplets, eerily hazed by the manufactured car lights. A little wind gusted in the breezy rain, hinting at an ominous, cloud-filled sky above—one I couldn't see or particularly cared to view. Clear nights and luminous stars seemed a far-distant galaxy away. It's no road for ancient starlight at the moment, I thought. A wry smile flashed—or maybe it didn't—as I accelerated away.

After a while, the rhythm of windscreen wipers beating away the rain and the drone of a podcast sedated me somewhat. True stillness and peace evaded me, and no milky moonlight seeped into the valley. I grimaced—or I hope I did—and drove on into the rain and into the night.

How many raindrops fall into the lightless valley unnoticed by anyone?

Almost all of them, I surmised.

My eyes were dry, and I in need of a river of tears to boat me out of this faraway fucking place.

Thoughts from a Country Hospital

Another week is nearly banked away to the annals of time and sure devil the bit have I written about its passing. I've expended much labour over the summer months pursuing numerous explorations of mind, spirit and emotion; some useful and some downright bonkers.

However, with the arrival of September's autumnal tinting of the lights and shades in the world, my physical bag of bones decided it had quite enough of my incessant digital blatherings and insisted on some tender loving care. Grabbing my attention in a most eye-catching manner by booking me in for an open-ended retreat at a country hospital in the west of Ireland. So, here I lay, a few days in, soaking up the rays on a mechanical bed from a sun peeking in through a curtainless window.

It's been an interesting experience to be unexpectedly flung into the Irish health system. Actually, let me try that sentence again. It has been an interesting experience to be unexpectedly flung into a system, and forced to exist in a specific manner, with a plethora of rules. I'm happy to report, though, my round peg seems even larger than the last time I attempted to squeeze it into a shrinking square hole.

My sudden vacation began to manifest on Tuesday evening when I developed a shivering fever and a swelling of my right foot, more or less, simultaneously. Followed quickly by an intense period of crying for about twenty minutes. Now, if I have worried over anything—symptom-wise—over the last three days it's been about the oddity of those particular tears. I seemed misted by a profound and deep sadness but a sorrow somehow alien to my senses; as if the tears and emotion felt were not altogether my own. Then again, I was quite deliriously drunk with fever, so perhaps the episode was a hallucination of sorts. But I think not.

On eventual arrival into the hospital environment, I was greeted at reception by a number of the 'Da Covid' questions which was a mite astonishing at over two years remove from the height of that era of banana-flavoured oddness. In hindsight, I should have answered this particular set of questions dishonestly and saved myself a bundle of aggravation.

I'm not sure if my unvaxxed status set off a series of alarm bells on the Irish health service's antiquated computer systems or not, but in the past thirty-six hours I've had two different sets of students, one nursing and one medical, approach me with requests for help—via surveys—in furthering their education about me. The central theme of both pleas was a trawl through my entire family medical history. I politely declined but was tempted to pass on the landline phone number of our clan's chief medical officer—my mother—who would happily fill a few copybooks worth of blow-by-blow accounts for the trainee medics, highlighting the major medical, psychological and psychiatric conditions prevalent in our family oak tree and the mountainous number of cunts in the North Galway environment who might well be the root cause of most of them.

The makeup of the workforce in this country hospital is broadly in line with my historic writing on the subject. Majority non-Irish. It's been a very good experience for me to get the opportunity to observe the personal side and nature of some of the people toiling away in a health system I criticise so frequently. Although, to be fair, anything I write on the current affairs front is usually targeted at policy or an agenda at play by the nefarious governing forces rather than the everyday people caught up in the spider web.

The night staff seem mostly made up of Indian nurses thus far and they have a grand gentleness and femininity about them as they go about their night-to-night business quietly and efficiently. Exotic fragrances scent the air as they enter the darkened room to empty or replace the antibiotics at the end of my intravenous drip. The day nurse is an African woman, and she announces herself to our small ward in the morning as follows:

'Good morning, boys, I am your nurse for the day.'

A cool, comforting directness and touch of masculinity replacing the watchful and protective femininity of the night. The elderly patient and retired farmer to my left loves the Irish nurses, as one might expect, as most are up for having the bit of craic and laughter with him and instinctively know how to massage the cold systems of care, just enough, to tailor them to his needs and personality. This uniquely Irish ability to carry out their duties with professionalism and authority and yet somehow also allow themselves to be treated like granddaughters by their patients. An umbilical link of understanding, perhaps, between one generation of green-eyed fairies and the next. Unspoken but speaking volumes too.

Yesterday, that is to say Thursday, felt a strange day. One with a foot in two different worlds—excuse the pun. This is explained, in the first instance, by a temperature that remained a touch above normal all day. Sleep and pure tiredness came in short bursts throughout the day and night. After waking up at 1 am, and a restless hour tossing and turning in the bed, at 2 am, I decided to go down to pay Brigid a nocturnal visit in the car park. An opportunity to reflect on all that had happened and so quickly too. While puffing on a smoke I randomly sampled a sentence. Indeed, I've tested it out a number of times over the last couple of days, in various states of pain and mental fog. It feels consistently true to me across all examinations so far.

I have no fear of dying.

Not that I'm in imminent danger or anything.

Obviously, I'd prefer my next visit to Corrib Oil didn't involve being spray-gunned with five litres of petrol and going up in a ball of over-caffeinated flames but I'm at ease if my end-of-shelf-life date is tomorrow. This is a new development in my psychological make-up, one which seems to have crept up on me unnoticed.

Death has always played a prominent role in my mind-space. I've always felt, from a young age, that I'm running out of time. This fear usually triggers a secondary concern—the amount of my life I've already wasted. At some point over the last couple of years I've lost these fears, which pleases me.

Now, the new revelation doesn't mean I'll be immediately transferred from this life to some grassy, sunlit savannah of heaven. No, rather that I'm at peace with the thought of sitting down to answer for the life I've lived if needs be. It will be a difficult, difficult conversation but one I'm open to having now with Himself. There is a certain serenity to discover death has no real hold over me anymore. But it raises another question.

'Do I have no fear of living?'

Hmmm. On first fly-by consideration, a positive answer isn't as confidently bounding out of my soul. And that might be one of the lessons of the last few days. Perhaps, death will come when all of my fears of living have been conquered and at that precise point I might well discover the difference between life and death may only be the spelling of the words on the page.

The specialist in charge of my foot is an Irish doctor and a woman of early middle-age. She arrived in the morning with a gaggle of learner ducklings in tow, and all huddled for a few minutes around my swollen right hoof. From all of my interactions with her so far she seems very competent and speaks knowingly on the subject of cellulitis to me and her gathered flock. She's a little concerned that the swelling hasn't started to recede a little more, but no new gains have been made into the enemy territory above my ankle. So, all told, not too bad, I suppose. She eyes me for a couple of seconds towards the end of this morning's little chinwag, wondering aloud if I'm keeping the foot properly elevated and rested—a note of genuine concern in her voice. She advised that an ultrasound needed to be undertaken later in the day and that my country retreat was likely to last a few days more.

I was tempted to reassure her that my hops out of the ward for cigarette breaks were being kept to a minimum and that Brigid has only driven to the cappuccino machine at Corrib Oil, a mile up the road, twice since I've been admitted to her fine establishment. But, alas, I got bitten by the laryngitis epidemic currently gusting through the corridors of pain and injury outside Room No. 60.

On their exit, and after breakfast, I sat down in the armchair to have a think and wee chat with myself. I couldn't ignore the inconvenient fact that all in this hospital environment were doing everything one could ask of them to heal my foot. Scientifically speaking. Perhaps, while the medical staff deal with my disease, I need to focus on the intense, short-lived sadness that announced its full arrival.

When I began the current phase of my life, a little over fifteen months ago, it kicked off unexpectedly in a cathedral. As written previously, I wrote a simple intention in a book of prayers seeking forgiveness from the people I'd hurt and perhaps might hurt in the future. Words written casually, absent-mindedly and in lieu of something truly specific to say. Thirty minutes later I felt that forgiveness from the divine in a most uncasual, unexpected and powerful way. In short, from a God I didn't really think about or really believe in for most of my life. I was a divine fence sitter.

As I think about that moment now, along with the most recent one on my couch, they had a similar feel and texture to them but were not identical. We often obsess about the hurt we've inflicted on others and it comes with no little shame and self-loathing. Anyone reading this who's been to an AA meeting will understand what I am talking about here. So, it can be a natural course of events, especially for people with addictive personality types on the road to recovery, like my good self, to obsess on past mistakes, past moments and past shames. Nothing wrong with a healthy amount of this type of reflection but what we are not addicted to, so easily, is forgiving the people who have hurt us. Whether that be in past times or, who knows, even during past lives. Often this number is a tiny collective of people but a very significant group nonetheless. A consideration flies by the drip stand as I chew the cud on all of this.

Have I ever considered that some of these people are profoundly sorry for having hurt me?

So sad, in fact, that they will never find the words of apology in this life. Further, maybe this was an emotion echoing from ages long past and a family tree that those medical and nursing students were so interested in learning about earlier in the day and yesterday. But, regardless of the origin point, the sorrow exists and is yearning for the calming balm of someone's forgiveness. A tear drops from my eye at this hopeful thought.

Internally, I intensely reject putting names and faces to the small number of people who've hurt me in my life which I believe is an entirely healthy state of affairs most of the time. But residual hurt exists in me, and probably in most of us, and so perhaps this flood of sadness last Tuesday was an apology of sorts and if it was, and having felt it, I now know, instinctively, that words, phrases or essays of apology would never have convinced the doubting Thomas in me on their own. Maybe the hurt accumulated in my foot is both medical and spiritual in nature, and while the antibiotics work their magic, I too have a job of work to complete and should use this time away to no longer postpone the release of these bruises from the past.

A Recovering Masculine

Operation Wounded Paw is winding down nicely and my right foot is on the mend, or at least isn't as angry-looking anymore. I understand that my resistance warrior credentials have taken a major hit after admitting to partaking in a little traditional medicine and intravenous antibiotics. But fear not, I'm currently glugging down some chlorine dioxide and some other off-beat remedies. Furthermore, on escape from the clutches of Portiuncula Hospital my first port of call was to dip my feet in the healing waters of Lough Nafooey up in the wild hills of Finny.

I wanted to wait until I was well out of hospital before chatting about my fellow ward inmate. My next-door neighbour, or comharsa béal dorais as we say in the native tongue, was an elderly gentleman who we shall refer to as Larry for the purposes of anonymity. Larry and I had a few wonderful conversations during my stay but even more importantly some marvellous silences too. He was a mighty man to be wordless around.

If synchronised silence ever becomes an Olympic sport, I'd fancy our chances together. I often wonder if finding someone who is at peace with your shut mouth is more vital than searching for people compatible with your open one—the actual secret sauce to creating a happy and peaceful existence, perhaps.

Anyway, Larry and I would often chatter away busily for fifteen minutes and then drift off into the private domains of our minds for an hour or two. Only to return again and pick up the conversation right where we left it. No hurt feelings, judgement or emotional neediness at play. As far as I could tell, the masculine and feminine were as finely balanced in his being as I've come across in quite a while.

He was both a soft man and a hardy man. I put this curiosity, in part, down to a life lived on the land in partnership with a wife he clearly still adored as much as his fields, even at ten years' remove from her passing to the next world. He'd flick her name into conversation when talking about the things he loved doing like farming, football and gardening. As if adding a little salt and slab of butter to a plate of fatty bacon and spuds just so he could catch the pleasant aroma and taste of her once or twice a day.

He was a great man for the nicknames and each morning he cheerfully greeted the young trainee male nurse taking bloods as the Ahascragh Vampire. I was the Lone Ranger due to my inability to lie still and remain on the ward for more than thirty minutes at a time and my stubborn refusal to allow visitors into the hospital. I had a rationale for this latter point, although he wasn't buying my story in the least.

'Ah now, take it from an old man on his own. The older you get the more you realise life's much better when you're not sharing it alone.'

Aye, aye, Captain.

Now, Larry, on the other hand, could run for president with the number of people enquiring after his well-being. After a couple of days of shadow-boxing, a light cloud of comfort, ease and good humour enveloped our two beds. I'd normally be the first to wake and by the time I'd be back from my first intravenous cigarette trip of the day, Larry would be stirring in the leaba beside me and putting a brave face on the indignity of having his nappy changed.

'Jaysus, you're still alive, Larry. I was looking forward to having two breakfasts for meself this morning.'

'Still above ground, still above ground,' he'd reply with a quiet, determined smile.

I suppose, reminiscing about Larry now gets me pondering on matters of intimacy. It seems a funny thing but the longer you travel on the road of life and build up scar tissue, the more difficult emotional intimacy with people can be to develop. Go so far, but no further. Whether those people be old or new. I guess it depends on how well each deals with the scars scratched into their skin.

As we paddle along our lives we adopt and accept roles, functions, labels, and dare I say it, masks to the world around us. The hospital environment was a revelation of sorts in this regard. It is one of the few environments where I've been thrown into close proximity with another person at random for an extended period of time. I had no choice in the matter. Strangely, emotional intimacy came naturally with Larry. As I analyse why this was, I come to the conclusion it was because, in the first instance, Larry didn't matter to me and I didn't matter to him. I was not invested in his life before I entered hospital and won't be in the future now that I am out of it. Yet, as I sit here now, I can see somehow Larry mattered a great deal indeed.

Larry was popular, and his old flip phone chirped regularly each day with well-wishers enquiring after his gall bladder. On Sunday, he confided the news that his sickness was noted at the Saturday night Mass from the altar which he was happy to hear about. A sign and a relief to him, and many of his generation, that he is a cherished member of his community whose sickness should be marked and prayed upon.

'I'm not into religion but sure it doesn't kill anyone to spend thirty minutes a week saying the odd prayer and giving thanks, does it?'

A practical, logical brand of faith which made me smile by its sheer honest simplicity. His son, daughters, relatives and others dropped in to visit him every day. Yet, his demeanour would often change, ever so slightly, to the one I came to observe as he adopted his role as father, retired farmer, and goodly neighbour. Sometimes our nearest and dearest know so much about us and yet nothing at all about what ticks underneath.

I liked Larry because his warmth and softness cushioned his strength. Although in his early eighties he was and is a strong man. His more traditionally male characteristics needed no formal introduction. You'd bump into them when needed and at the appropriate time. All told, he'd a lovely balance and humour to him—or so it seemed to me.

When I think of spirit and faith in terms of energy, and split these fields into the precise make-up each and every one of us possesses of masculine and feminine characteristics, I come to a surprising observation about myself. The feminine energy is the dominant sphere, and that is probably due to collateral damage to the masculine in me at points along the road. I'm most comfortable and at peace operating within a spectrum of intuition, empathy, and creativity. The damaged masculine in me will sabotage these states of being at times, and I can knee-jerk into many toxic male traits at the flick of a switch—but which are nowadays mostly confined to the interior of my car and the altar of Brigid as often as possible. But maybe I should let Larry and others I meet along the way be the teachers and judges of those self observations.

A recuperating masculine saddled with a recovering alcoholic.

A Little Beauty in the Beast

I'll let you into a secret. When I started a recent boot camp for body and soul, it was a light-hearted attempt to lose a little weight, inject more exercise into my daily routine, and write with a touch more spiritual consideration and focus. A little reflective pause until I figured out exactly what to spend the rest of my fucking life scribbling about. Nice plan, but it ain't exactly worked out that way so far.

For example, as a Weight Watchers enterprise, it's been a complete disaster. If followed as a clean-living and eating programme, the marketing material might read as follows:

'Roll up, roll up, come in chunky and we guarantee you'll go out morbidly obese after forty days—or your money back.'

In addition, the spirit side of the house has been quite the rollercoaster, as some who've been travelling this road with me through recent episodes may have noticed. So, on that front, let me tell you about yesterday, and by way of introduction, I'll need to start with the day before.

After nearly three weeks, I was once more able—finally—to sit down and type for fifteen or sixteen hours in one sitting. When I say one sitting, I mean a sitting with twenty cigarette and tea breaks and a contemplative spin with Brigid on the motorway, but one overall writing session. Which, believe it or not, is my happy place. During this process I don't talk, surf social media, respond to texts or answer the phone.

So, in essence, I re-found my ability to hold an overall mood and explore a couple of emotional pitches for sixteen hours. For good or ill. I'm not someone who can write three or four paragraphs and wait two days for more enlightenment to shuffle along in my direction and then proceed on, because I'll never recover precisely the original mood and exploratory pitch. If that makes any sense—and it probably doesn't.

When I completed my writing assignment, at about 4:30 am, I was pretty much in love with myself and relieved. I tried to sleep but drowsiness escaped me. Eventually, I decided to go for a drive with no specific destination in mind. Well, maybe that's not quite true. My conscious mind had no idea where I was going, but I suspect my subconscious knew exactly where to steer the wheel. I'm more and more convinced it triggers patterns and rituals I'm only now becoming vaguely aware of. Both short term and long term ones. Anyway, forty minutes later I was walking into the church of St Mary of the Holy Rosary in Cong on the grounds of Cong Abbey. I've often ended up in this holy land over the last six months.

About ten days after I inherited Brigid, I found myself in the same church offering up prayers. On that occasion, when I stood up to leave and turned slightly round, there on the wall behind me was an old-style St Bridget's cross made from straw or reeds. I'd never noticed it on previous visits to the church. I take these odd synchronicities to mean something nowadays. A divine signpost, perhaps. A signal with no lettering and not pointing in any definitive direction, but a sign merely that I've found one. Offering hope a path is out there, somewhere, for me to follow. I remember being anxious and worried in advance of that visit, and the sight of the cross calmed me a little.

On yesterday's visit, though, I was peaceful and filled with a rich sense of gratitude. I was happy to kneel and pray and not to fight my usual urge to just rifle through a few decades of the Rosary and leave. A few tourists came and went. I observed the beautiful stained-glass windows behind the altar and drank in some more tranquillity. After a while, I got up and ambled across to the Hungry Monk Café and ordered a coffee to go.

To go where, though?

I climbed back into the car and drifted out of the village, and instead of taking a right for Ballinrobe and back to Tuam and home, Brigid kept cruising straight towards Clonbur. My conscious mind soon twigged on to what my subconscious had already mapped out. I was setting sail for Lough Nafooey near Finny via the back roads. I was a little confused but drank my coffee and lit a smoke. Recent trips to Lough Nafooey were usually accompanied by much inner turbulence, but I was feeling at peace with the world yesterday. I took my time and enjoyed the spin. The sky was filled with clouds of different whites and light greys, and the day was warm.

About five years ago, Lough Nafooey, although miles from any proper civilisation, was a popular tourist destination for day-trippers living in Galway and Mayo. People could drive a car or even camper van onto the land behind the beach, and find a spot to park, hitch a tent, or have a barbeque and swim in the glacially cool waters.

However, a fire, at some point during the pandemic, or soon after, put paid to many of those activities. A steel gate now blocks the entrance and all access to the lough is on foot. The by-road snaking the western side of the lake leading to this entrance is too narrow to afford people many parking opportunities on the side of the road. As a result, the numbers visiting the place seem to have dwindled away quite significantly in the last couple of years.

On arrival, the place was deserted, and I quite easily found somewhere to abandon the car. I swung through the steel pedestrian gate and a single sheep was waiting to greet me from the middle of the muddy track leading to the beach. I wasn't sure whether it was a ewe or a ram, and it didn't look particularly bothered whether I figured it out or not. I decided I was in the presence of a ewe and trotted along. Her mangled, knotty horns were fully grown, and a fluffy, woolly fleece in need of shearing provided protection from the elements. She turned and trotted back to her day as I passed by and branched off for the beach.

I walked up and down the natural orangey-yellow sands and gulped in my surroundings. This area has seen not just glacial times but volcanic ones too, and I wondered if this might explain the uniqueness and beauty of the coarse sands beneath my feet. The area surrounding Lough Nafooey is the stomping ground of the ancient Finny volcano, whose birthing is recorded in geological tomes as occurring 490 million years ago, or at roughly the same time as Pat McDonagh introduced the first smokey-bacon burger at Supermac's in the occasionally lava-erupting Ballinasloe. Not many people know that.

Eventually, I stood still on the beach and gazed out at the beauty of the calm lake waters and began to pray. I don't engage in formalised prayer, generally speaking, at Lough Nafooey. No 'Our Fathers', 'Hail Marys', or 'Glory Be' prayers. I just begin talking to Himself or trying to feel the presence of the Holy Spirit in my ageing bones. More often searching for the latter, actually.

As an aside, I'm slowly making my way through volumes one and two of Paramahansa Yogananda's writings called 'The Second Coming of Christ'—a revelatory commentary on the original teachings of Jesus. One of the things I enjoy about reading it is the description of the Holy Spirit as 'Christ Consciousness'. The wording resonates for me when thinking of the Holy Spirit in this way—as a consciousness existing all around and within us too. Or like a restful lake I might step into and be transfigured into a divine reality once I muster up a little intestinal fortitude and dip my head beneath the cool waters.

Yesterday, all I really wanted to say was thank you. Appreciation for the respite from weeks of torment. Almost immediately, my eyes began to water. As if I'd stumbled into a dusty room at the end of a long, dark corridor only to discover it was the very place all of my joy and beauty resided in. Long waiting for me to take a peek. All of a sudden, it felt as if what I was feeling inside mirrored exactly the beauty of Lough Nafooey and the mountains surrounding it. For a few fleeting moments I was part of the gorgeousness and it was part of me. This sense of belonging, if that is the correct phrase, pulsed thunderously powerful. I felt the urge to tell someone, but fortunately the beach was empty except for the lone sheep now patrolling the lake shore. For what indeed would I have said if I happened upon someone out for a leisurely stroll?

'Hey, you there, have you any fucking idea of how beautiful you are—all of us are?'

A wide-eyed, manic outburst as likely to lead to the men with white jackets sprinting in my direction as anything else. Yet, a little sun broke through the puffy clouds at that moment, indicating to me divine truth was present in the air. My peace stretched a little longer.

I like to believe each of us has our own ray of sunlight lighting a path to the sun. The ray often disappears, masked by clouds and mists. The path teems with rains of discouragement and winds of distraction and my own sin. A road invisible to the naked eye more often than not. But, every once in a month of Sundays, you inadvertently feel the way to the next sunburst. I think that's what happened yesterday. Of course, the feeling of oneness passed into memory before I hit the Corrib Oil in Ballinrobe for another coffee, and some ugliness within and without slowly seeped back into my world. But near home, it dawned on me that, by escaping my boot camp, I'd stumbled into a boot-camp day organically. If only I could manage to put a few more of them back-to-back.

One fact remains with me, though, I believe.

I won't be able to think and lie my way out of the truth, the truth of what inner beauty feels like because I accidentally tripped over it yesterday for a few short moments. And if it's hidden away there in someone as ungodly as me, well, the rest of you reading this might be a bunch of beautiful fuckers too.

One Enchanted Moment

- a short story on healing

It was the night after Christmas and the man sat on a fallen oak in a forest kingdom that they said was protected by the Tuatha Dé, the tribe of old myth and spirit. The trunk of the felled tree was wide and bridged across a narrow but deep gurgling river that dissected the ancient heart-shaped woodland in two. The waters below were dark, or seemed so to the man. Soft moss carpeted the decaying tree on both sides of the river, blanketing the bark snugly into the bed of frosted undergrowth.

Earlier, the man had followed the path of this stream to the fallen tree, for it was the shortest and surest route into and out of the enchanted wood and his appointment with the wise man. With the aid of the softly cushioning moss underfoot, the man had easily hopped up onto the trunk of the oak and then proceeded to walk carefully across its length before fixing himself down at the centre point of both the fallen tree and the river below. When all was done, his black-booted feet hung just a couple of metres above the dark waters, with the laces of one dangling closer still to the darkness below.

There was nothing for him to do but wait. Wait for his enchanted moment.

The night was dark, but the sky was clear. A few stars peeked out, here and there. As the man sat and bided his time, he began to trace the contours of the river with his eyes. Soon, they were attuned to the blackness all around him. The river tracked north in perfect alignment with Polaris, the northern star. The river-path allowed for a natural break from the density of trees elsewhere in the forest, and so a small patch of sky could be viewed clearly from the man's seat on the tree. This patch of sky was moonless, but that was to be expected and a sign he was not late. The man paused to check his timepiece and nodded slowly to himself.

Almost time.

It was the night of an Ghealach Fhuar, the Cold Moon, the last full moon of the year. Indeed, the last full moon of the old world. It was out there somewhere, he thought, just not arrived yet into view. The man glanced to his left and then to his right and caught glimpses of pale moonshine breaking through the woodland canopy. Flickering moonlight illuminating thick leafless branches and the mossy carpets of frosted ground below. The branches in turn cast their own shadows and cloaked other areas into complete darkness.

The man looked down at his dangling feet and the gently babbling stream. The sound of it, a hypnotic music, almost inviting and seducing the man's ears and senses. He thought back to the sadness of the past and wondered how to leap forward into the future alone and the new world approaching fast. He could see nothing and heard only the gentle melody of the waters beneath whispering to him to come closer. He closed his eyes and could feel a torrent welling within and emitted a tortured wheeze, and then another. It was a hissing and almost involuntary escape from lips jammed shut. Erupting emissions moments before the towering pressure inside choked him. A big salty tear sped down the side of his face and fell into the depths of the river—diving off from his chin. Another followed it. He nodded his head and opened his eyes once more.

Enough. Enough.

With his eyes adjusted to the shadows he looked down and noticed a silvery, moon-like image reflecting back into his eyes from the river below. Not the expected Cold Moon itself exactly, but rather the portrait of a boy smiling cheekily and making faces back to him from the waters. Startled, he momentarily lost balance and started sliding helplessly off the old wooden trunk. Then, almost immediately, and at the one time, a voice called out as a steely arm encircled his waist and easily pulled him back up onto the tree.

'I've got you,' the wise man said simply.

The man turned to drink in the apparition now sitting by his side on the fallen trunk. Grateful, embarrassed, and infinitely so.

'I got lost in meself for a minute, and almost drifted away,' the man murmured in formal thanks with a little shamefacedness sprinkled in and bowed his head. As he tried to compose himself, he looked up again and a little closer at the wise man. His fine grey whiskers and dishevelled goatee were bathed in moonlight. His grey eyes filled with humble sagacity and a little mischief too, he thought.

'We all get a little lost in ourselves, sure, don't we?' the wise man replied. He smiled and slapped himself a couple of times on the forehead. There was neither question nor answer in his words. He settled into the silence of the night and lit a Sweet Afton. After a couple of minutes, the wise man's quietness began to unsettle the man, for he had much to get off his chest and only a forest gap's worth of moonlit sky in which to do it. If he could even do it.

'I might not make it to the new world,' blurted out the man.

Embarrassed, he stopped abruptly in mid-sentence and was immediately sorry for his own hopeless admission. He retreated to wordlessness and surrendered himself to it completely. Once again, attempting to leave behind the tyrannical clouds of his mind for a while. He glanced up to the newly appeared full moon and then placed the palms of his hands face-down on either side of his waist on the cool bark, and relaxed back a little into the stillness. In a twinkling, the shivering Cold Moon glistened a refreshing balm down on his worried and emotion-filled features. Both men closed their eyes to soak in the moonlight and peace.

After a while, though, the man's thoughts began to stir from their slumber again and moved across into the calm patch of sky he had found. He could feel his old shadows fighting to make a reappearance.

'Are we waiting for someone?' asked the man as gently as he could. The wise man opened his lids and grinned, then his shoulders began to shudder as his smile turned into laughter. Soon, his great bellowing echoed across the forest, a most beautiful noise if quite unexpected. Birds tittered, the woodland animals guffawed, and a tawny old owl hooted his amusement. As the symphony of merriment chorused together, the man's frozen anger thawed and rose like mercury, as if it were suddenly the hottest of days and not the coolest of nights.

'Are me darkest shadow and worries a laughing stock, old man, is that it?' the man erupted angrily.

All in the forest fell quiet as if the sound of a gunshot had unexpectedly reverberated across the night. The wise man said nothing, but a spark of devilment still rolled around in his eyes. The moon shifted to the centre of the sky in the tree-gap in front of them, shining its most brilliant silvery-white light. Suddenly, the giggling of children could be heard all around them. The man swivelled his head, this way and that, but could not spy a sinner in sight. But, after a moment more, something instantly whizzed by his head, a small object of some kind, although the man failed to see it. And then again.

Phizzzzzzzz…

On the third hearing, the man felt a sharp sting on the side of his cheek. Instinctively, he crouched his shoulders, lowered his head, and his hands flashed up to his face to touch the wound but also protect himself from further attacks.

'Yes! Got him, I got him, yesssss…' a young boy's voice cried out in triumph.

Before the man could radar in on the location of the voice, a young brown-haired boy of freckled face stepped out from behind a single line of silver-barked birch trees. These trees overlooked the stream to the right of where the two men were situated. Unbelievably, the boy was a mere matter of yards away when he chose to reveal himself. He strutted triumphantly towards the fallen oak and lightly hopped up and made his way across to them.

'Haha. Mister, you weren't expecting me, were you?—I was closer to you than you thought, wasn't I?' the boy chuckled out as he took a seat down beside the two. Drawing his knees up towards his chin and then wrapping his arms around his long, lithe legs, before finally interlocking his fingers together to seal himself snugly into place. He easily rested his chin idly onto one of his kneecaps, pure delighted with himself.

'That hurt, young fella, you shouldn't be darting around the forest in the shadows, laughing at me problems. You might have your own one day,' admonished the man.

'Is that right now?'

'Yeah, it is,' the man returned, a little huffily.

'And tell me now, Mister, how do you know I don't have problems of me own already?' the boy rifled back, his eyes filled with light humour and mischief as he relaxed his legs down into a proper sitting position. This freed up his mucky hands and he used one to idly scratch his head and began rooting around in his wild mesh of wiry brown hair as if he were looking for something. Soon, he removed a horse-chestnut. Nonchalantly, he eased an arm over his shoulder and pulled out the catapult hidden in his hooded vest. He loaded it with the horse-chestnut and took general aim at the crater-pocked moon ahead.

Phizzzzzzzz...

'Sure, what problems would a boy like you have scampering around the woods untamed and free?' the man enquired sternly. But his curiosity was piqued.

'Oh, I see, only your shadows from the age of men are important, and not any from the forest of the young, is that it?' the boy countered with a certain confident hint of knowing. As if he were the adult and the man were the child in this most odd of conversations.

The man was temporarily stumped by the question—on a forest floor littered with many stumps to choose from. He turned to the wise man for a sage interjection and some clarity on how to interact with the boy. The wise man seemed to have fallen into a light sleep, and a gentle snore was the only response to the man's enquiring eyes. He looked to the sky and could see the moon was already two-thirds across the gap in the forest heavens. The enchanted moment wouldn't last much longer, and he feared he might not get another one. It seemed that the only one to talk to about his problems was the unruly boy. A most unsatisfactory predicament, but the only one that remained open to him.

'I was a happy kid once, you know, not unlike you, in fact. You don't know how lucky you are, young fella,' he began.

'Is that right?' smiled the boy before pinging another horse-chestnut into the face of the moon. The man shook his head in disappointment and could see the boy wasn't taking him too seriously.

'It wasn't right what happened. I was hurted. Hurted badly!' he shot back defensively.

'You were hurted now, were you?' the boy laughed sardonically, before phizzing yet another horse-chestnut into a crater on the moon.

'I feckin' was, but I suppose you're too innocent and immature to understand these things, young fella. I'm carrying this burden round a long time now,' he answered sadly but with a little pride too.

'You're carrying a child on your back all these years, is that it?'

'Protecting him,' he responded with a little heat. The boy started to giggle again.

'What would a little garsún like you know about it anyways. All you have to carry around is that catapult and a few horse-chestnuts?' he followed on.

At this the boy side-turned to the man and handed him the catapult, and excavated a horse-chestnut from his wiry mane and placed it in the man's hand too.

'Why don't you have a go?'

The man looked down at the catapult and considered the daftness of the request. Eventually, he decided that although he had nothing to gain, he also had nothing to lose in this situation. Illogically, something stirred deep inside him that caused him to tighten his grip on the simple piece of wood. He nestled the horse-chestnut into the thick rubber band and pulled it back.

'That's it, that's it. Keep pulling it back!' said the boy encouragingly .

The man did as he was told and pulled the rubber band back until it was almost taut, and he momentarily worried he might break it.

'What now?' he asked, taking a sideways glance at the boy.

'Take aim at the moon, Mister, and very, very quickly let go,' the boy advised.

'The moon... and let go?' he repeated.

'Yes. Just. Let. Go.' The boy smiled in boyish wisdom and locked eyes with the man.

'That's the most important bit. Do you think you can do that, Mister?' the boy wondered aloud while maintaining his eye connection with the man.

The man took a deep breath, and then another. And then a faint phizzing noise could be heard as another horse-chestnut rocketed into the edge of the moon. The man put out his hand for another horse-chestnut, and the boy happily placed one into it. He visibly relaxed, enjoying the release of childish energy. The boy kept handing him horse-chestnuts and the man kept pelting them at the moon.

'I'm sorry for my outburst and not taking your problems seriously,' he said after a while.

'Ah, that's okay, Mister,' the boy replied quietly.

'Do you have any real problems, though? You seem so carefree?' the man asked, now genuinely interested to know. The boy's happy countenance began to turn to shadow and he nodded his head slowly and a little painfully.

'Ah, I do, Mister. You wouldn't believe this now, but I've a man sitting on me shoulders all the time weighing me down.'

'Really?' the man replied.

'The older he gets, the heavier his burden. He's killing me slowly, I fear,' the boy whispered sadly.

'What! You must be joking. Come on now. Really?'

The last of the boy's good humour drained from his face and he nodded his head up and down sadly in answer. The man was outraged and it immediately spiked a fire of volcanic anger inside him as he thought back to his own shadow and treatment as a lad.

'Let me help. I promise I can help you!' the man begged and cried out.

'Is that right?' the boy answered, the trace of a despondent smile filling his face.

'Yes, yes, of course. What can I do?' he assured him.

'You could climb down off my back—I'd like to leave this forest one day,' the boy whispered slowly, his eyes dropping to the dark waters below his feet.

The moon inched towards the very edge of the gap in the trees. Soon, it would disappear from sight, but the stillness of its light was at its most powerful. The silence devoured every cloud in the sky, both seen and unseen. Horrifying realisation flooded the man's senses. No little guilt too. He soaked the boy's words into every shred of his being. After a few moments more, the man calmly returned the catapult to the boy's hood and gently engulfed his small, dirty hand into the heart of his own. He locked eyes with him once more.

'I can do that, I think. I can really do that...' he said. Although no words were exchanged. A smile broke out from behind the boy's quiet tears and lit across his freckled face and brown eyes as the man held the boy's gaze with the strength of his promise. They remained frozen like this for a long spell of time and healing. A duration timeless in nature. Until, quite suddenly, the wise man's words broke their voiceless conversation.

'Ah, I see you two have met properly then?' he intoned.

The man nodded vigorously and the boy giggled.

'What do we do now, though?' asked the man.

The wise man pointed to the edge of the riverbank to a place under the canopy of the silver birch trees. Not more than a few feet away.

'There's an old raft down there. Have you not seen it?' the wise man replied in puzzlement.

The man and the boy quickly turned their attention in the direction the wise man was pointing to below them. And there it was, illuminated in the moonlight. Old, sturdy tree branches of varying lengths and tree types knotted together with a long blue rope. The boy jumped up excitedly onto the oak trunk and in an instant somersaulted from his place on the oak onto the raft. Then turned back to the men on the tree-bridge.

'How come I never saw this before?' he shouted up to them in pure joy.

Instead of replying to the boy the wise man swivelled towards the man in answer.

'Sometimes, it takes quite a journey for the eyes to see.'

The man smiled in new knowing and he too began to laugh. He edged across the trunk to hug the wise man in a warm embrace.

'Well, are you going to join your young friend on the raft?' enquired the old man.

The man paused and looked down on the raft. The young lad was on his knees whistling to himself and testing the sturdiness of the branches tied together binding the raft in place. His heart was bursting with love at the carefree sight of him. A final tear dropped into the river.

'You'll make sure he makes it to the new world, won't you?' the man eventually replied.

The wise man nodded his head slowly and the trace of a smile began to spread across his whiskers. Gingerly he straightened himself into a standing position and began walking across to the riverbank to join the boy on the raft. He bent down and picked up two long oak branches lying on the frozen ground and then hopped onto the raft. He put his arm around the boy's shoulder and both of them waved goodbye to the man. He gave a branch to the boy and moved to the back of the raft. Automatically, the boy took position at the front and other side of the raft. The boy turned one last time and with his free hand removed the catapult from his hood and dropped it into the stream.

'Good-bye, Mister!' he shouted up to the fallen oak in gratitude. Then, the wise man eased the raft away from the bank with his frosted oar and the two began to carefully paddle out of the heart-shaped prison.

In another instant, an Ghealach Fhuar passed from sight and the forest was plunged into darkness. There was a sun out there somewhere rising on a new world and the man was certain the boy would find it.

The Secrets of an Island

I jumped into the car and Brigid pointed us in the direction of sea and water. The pair of us on the hunt for a day of complete serenity, far from the seductions of my digital landscape. Omey, or Iomaí, is an island separated from mainland Connemara, and the Atlantic coast of Galway by a causeway of close to a kilometre in length. At low tide, nature opens her arms wide and handsome in a majestic *Céad Míle Fáilte* to allow lucky visitors access to the secrets of the island on foot or by car. This parting of the sea waters is a portal to another world—a wildly natural one—and a brief window to explore the treasures she hides.

What follows are the sandy footprints of a single pair of feet during one such parting of the waves.

The birds flew low and fast over the island ground with the confidence of nineteenth-century landlords—rulers of all they surveyed. Somewhat welcoming, but certain of themselves too, and their inherent ownership rights. The dune-lands of the five-hundred-and-forty-acre island were pockmarked with hundreds and hundreds of rabbit holes.

Everywhere and anywhere.

Wild rabbits and Irish hares raced hither and thither across the top of the turf just north of Omey beach and close to St Feichín's well—an ancient holy well marked by a mound of stones and some crosses. The sky seemed blanketed by a singular grey—a mirror reflection of the blanket boglands of Claddaghduff and the nearby austerity of west Connemara's topography.

There was warmth and moisture in the air—and wind too. But the dark sea, crowned with frothy waves, thrashed against the granite shorelines. Their tempo quick and turbulent, but not quite sure what the skies above held in store. Rain and a storm, perhaps. Or possibly the clouds might yield to brightness and allow themselves to be tugged gently downwards into serenity by the surrounding ocean's patient depths. A few flecks of precipitation parachuted onto the grassy dunes and flowers, testing the terrain with salty kisses. It was a day swelling and heaving with uncertainty.

A between-worlds day.

The open dune-lands rose gently from the solitary road. Here and there, to left and right, granite boulders materialised on the landscape—flung from the belly of the Western Atlantic and as stony grey as the cloud cover above their impenetrable heads. Proud and stern and a reminder of the mighty power of nature. The wind was neither gentle nor billowing, and its sound a mere backing vocal to an island enchanted by the melody of birdsong and the scampering feet of hares. A solitary bumblebee circled overhead, conducting the orchestra.

The odd sight of a stranded settee cushion lying beneath a small pebble-dashed cliff offered comforting views of the sea and Cruagh Island in the distance. Cruagh looked craggy and filled with tall, jagged edges on its right-hand side—a sanctuary for only the most determined pirates, a gull seemed to whisper. A small fishing boat was anchored at the mouth of the narrow strait between the island and mainland.

The complete tranquillity of the natural noises seemed almost false. The stillness immense. This calm silence—balming passing breaths into quiet—refused to be ignored or denied. The vocal cords of the island and the beasts divinely vibrating to its will without question. A musicality that smiled knowingly at the folly of furious minds and speedy thought patterns—of any thought patterns, perhaps.

A pair of larks began rapid, low patrols above the shipwrecked settee cushion, bottoming out no more than a foot above the woolly head of the washed-up sponge lying on top of it before turning back and repeating the exercise drill. The echoing sound of the larks' flight pattern softly draughted in drowsiness and peaceful, wordless dreams.

After a time, a gentle light could be seen illuminating the backs of the thick grey clouds, hinting at a sun somewhere unseen. The rain held off, but the wind whistled up along the shore a little stronger. The larks, still on patrol, encouraged shoeless movement amongst the dune grasses and villages of rabbit holes. Holly-like clumps of prickly green grew in patches along the way—occasionally pricking the soles like a tuning fork, encouraging continued attunement to the sacredness underfoot and all around.

Back up towards the beach, and twenty paces behind St Feichín's well, a black iron bench looked out over the sea, offering more sightings of Cruagh and two other islands. The skies held grey and the aroma of raindrops loitered in the air, but the bench asked for pause and reflection—something deeper. On a different day, the sun might've begun its slow, long descent into a mid-June set. On this day, the colour of light was tinting, a shade or two, with silvery-ash hues.

The bench was sturdy but uncomfortable, and a couple of birds struggled in the mid-distance, flapping against the breeze over the foam of the sea inlet off to the left. Unexpectedly, though, three-quarters of the way across the small bay, the birds turned around. Abruptly changing their flight pattern and returning towards the rocky coast near St Feichín's well. The white aviators were transformed entirely with wind assistance. The brisk southerly breeze stilled their outstretched wings and glided them higher and faster—swooping them up and down at breakneck speed without the birds seeming to move at all. Until finally landing on a rocky piece of shoreline granite where a small flock of friends awaited their safe arrival—and then two more took off in their place.

A new view from the bench offered a slightly lightening grey peace—but a peace without truth, of this day or the days ahead. A rickety, unstable kind of peace. The colours kept moving and slowly changing, mesmerising and seducing the senses. Far out past the islands, the curious spectacle of a few rays of sunlight could be seen caressing the sea—yet without any sight of the sun from the bench's perspective. Still only cloud prevailed. The landscape asked for a patience that the flowers and the rabbits and the birds instinctively understood. The sounds of the island knew patience was merely a slowing down of time. The sun would come as surely as the changing of the wind.

Gradually, one after another, strands of gold lethargically brushed themselves onto the canvas in front of and behind Cruagh Island. Then, finally, high above the sea, a yellow oval face peeked out through the tiniest break in the grey. Every living thing basked in its warmth for a few seconds before it again disappeared.

The road back to the causeway was mapped with cottages old and somewhat new, but no smoke piped from the chimneys. The laneway was lined with barbed-wire fences atop stone walls on both sides. A couple of small birds hopped along one of the fences ten paces ahead, guiding the way off the island. On the final turn down to the beach, a new sight could be observed. The wide, sandy expanse of causeway had disappeared. Instead, the tall blue-headed directional posts lined up across the beach were now up to their necks in gently lapping water. The sun winked through once more from the heavens, this time grinning. The return drawbridge to the unnatural world shut firmly closed. A firm invitation to tarry longer on the island.

A turn left along the remaining island beach not yet succumbed to the sea revealed a graveyard—familiar Irish and Galway names were engraved on the headstones. An island long bereft and robbed of new households and people, or townlands filled with voices, had an interesting twist. The headstones revealed people still returned to the island to make their final escape from this world. The burial ground marked graves with recent dates—dates more recent than the last full-time inhabitant to leave the island in 1973. So, an island graveyard facing the mainland but a final resting place a million miles closer to the warm embrace of *Himself* too—most likely.

Beyond the graveyard, and a turn in the curvature of the island, the ground rose and then fell again. A few cows mooed here and there, sounding the way ahead. The high tide produced a temporary cove with granite blocks cut into the island for clothes, a coat, and a plastic bag, along with a magically created narrow sandy beach. The water here was cool but not cold and sloped gently downwards to waist height—crystal clear, invigorating, fresh, and life-giving. The breeze dialled into its towelling nature as a few house lights from Claddaghduff sparked to life. A temporary beach to simply be for a while or two.

The north-to-northwest shore of the island hugged close to the seventh-century monastery remains of St Feichín. The old walls of the church, hidden for centuries by protective layers of sand dunes until the early 1980s, reminded the passer-by of the ancientness of the island and the secrets and wisdom held beneath its sands.

The second circuit of the island eventually coaxed the old settee pillow into view for a second time. With it, a new appreciation of the soft sponge and tired colours. A colony of different birds sat near the shore, but a motley crew absent of larks second time round. Darkness dripped in, drop by drop, and enwrapped the old barroom cushion and its occupant in a comforting slumber.

Until the return of the larks and their winged tidings of a sea and its ebbing.

A Passenger to my Thoughts

I'm just relaxing and stretching out on the couch again. I'm quite surprised some university hasn't given me an honorary degree for this type of activity yet. I've burned a lot of rubber lately with Brigid and need a little time to process a few bits and pieces. Anyway, if you're enjoying the last burning embers of the Bank Holiday weekend, this piece shouldn't tax the brain cells too much—and if you have nothing better to do, read on, I guess.

I'm at the mixing desk, harmonising some old stories with current times on the sofa and listening to some up-tempo Irish music. At times, it is important to live life in full, vibrant colour, I feel. But then, at others, it's just as meaningful to luxuriate in memories of living those times—to unearth understandings that only hindsight hatches into life. Often, an old chapter breathes new learnings with the passage of time.

I suppose, with a bit of reflection, I can say that the last full-on physical fight I became embroiled in occurred when I was fourteen years of age, or thereabouts. I was trundling dejectedly off a football pitch about two hundred yards away from where I type these words here today. We had lost a game by a point or two.

A short distance ahead of me, two boys were laughing and joking with each other. They were good friends, and at least one was a fellow boarder in my school, as I recall. The trigger point for the eruption of temper was one I am still shame-faced about reliving in the present. One of the two lads fooling around was on my team, while the other had just been watching the match, I think. Not to put too fine a point on the situation—I completely and utterly lost the plot. I took a run and launched myself up on top of the back of my teammate and wrestled him to the ground before starting to beat seven shades of shit out of the smile streaked across his face. It wasn't pretty.

In the aftermath of these outbursts of temper, the usual suspects often savaged me internally—shame, self-hatred, and embarrassment. The boy I attacked is a middle-aged man now and lives in my general vicinity. I guess I'm at the stage of my digital and tech struggle where I can't remember large chunks of the things I've written down about the past and presented to the public. So, I'm not quite sure if I've recorded this moment of shame-history to print before. Anyhow, on the rare occasions I bump into this man on the street or in a shop, I still can't quite bring myself to look him fully in the eye. In the way my brain and body are wired, that is altogether the correct response. Yet, I still miss my volcanic temper and the energy it unleashed within.

I have really only fully lost control of my temper a couple of times since that moment, but I am aware enough to know it is still there—occasionally lurking into view. In a strange way, my temper gives me comfort, for I know when it goes, I absolutely have no care in the world about what happens next. That unpredictability can be quite intoxicating, not dissimilar to drunkenness in a way, so I try to steer far clear of the room of the house it resides in most of the time.

Rewatching this video clip from my past in my mind's eye sparks another old story about two traveller lads in the town who both shared the same name—Brian Ward—one of whom was quite famous locally as an amateur boxer—possibly mentioned before here too. One of the Brians was down in the local social welfare office and encountered a new arrival working behind the counter for the Department of Social Welfare who wasn't quite sure which Brian was before her seeking assistance.

'Which Brian are you? Is it Brian the fighter?' she enquired.

'Jaysus, no. I'm Brian the lover—I'm here to collect the children's allowance.'

So, the moral of tonight's ramblings so far, for me at least, is to keep the auld life pendulum swinging somewhere between the lives of Brian the Fighter and Brian the Lover. Anger is an important part of my make-up, I feel. I used it to fuel a fire to win, yet blanking it bred an acceptance of the secondary prize. Settling for scenarios where I don't completely lose. A weird type of unsatisfying middle-world.

I was quite big for my age back then, and it was around this period I began a long-term, romantic relationship with cigarettes. I reckon that should be the textbook definition of a teenage love story: a picture of someone smoking and looking off into the distance—kinda sexy, cool in the imagination, but ultimately a painting that might kill you in the end. I should warn—again—this is mostly an excuse to sit down, type, and empty some of my accumulated rubbish into some black bin bags for morning collection outside the front door.

Spring has brought longer evenings, and I've been chatting and meeting with people again. My imagination and production line of tin-pot ideas have kick-started into diesel-powered action after the winter recess and are keeping me busy.

Peculiarly, people seem consumed with how bad the Irish weather has been lately, as if it hasn't always been so. I must confess I haven't been paying attention too much. But, I suppose, I can make an unexpected patch of sun on the motorway stretch a long way most of the time—once the dark nights have receded a touch.

This morning I woke up lonesome for my silent self. Writing things down brings many bounties, but probably the primary one is silence. My mouth zips shut, and my thoughts settle into the driver's seat—overly confident, erratic, and unprocessed. Busy as a beehive but too unstill to make much sense of.

Most often, it can take a while to settle them down, categorise them, and stop them from careering off down the highway at breakneck speed on their own. The key to success—which I haven't quite mastered—is to plot out an eventual destination and then quietly pull in off the road and switch off the engine. I sometimes worry that one day my thoughts will refuse to return the keys of my car. But today, I shudder away such sad visions and relax into the passenger seat. Surrendering to the keyboard, I'm excited by the places we might visit and discoveries we might make out on the road together.

A Summons to Knock

Last Sunday, as I eased my arse into the driver's seat, I was spiritually interrupted. Peering out through the mud-splattered windscreen, my attention couldn't escape the spectacle of a midday sun engaged in a bitter duel with some devilish-looking clouds. Sharp darts of radiance blazed into my eyes once or twice, then vanished, before making a beaming return.

With the advent of Brigid, the sun is a growing feature of my spiritual path. Himself makes use of it to announce his presence to me from time to time. So, unexpected appearances of shafts of blistering sunlight or a shiver of moonlight that coincide with a specific thought are a sort of divine indicator I pay attention to more and more. Daft as that may sound.

On this day, I was en route to the local police station to pick up a court summons, no less. For some type of speeding offence, I should add, and not any far-right literary activity—which was a little disappointing and ego-deflating. However, I interpreted the sky wars at play above the roof of my car to be heavenly instruction to ignore the summons of Lego-town functionaries for the afternoon.

So, instead, I instinctively rededicated the afternoon to observing the struggle between light and darkness at play over the villages and towns of north Galway and south Mayo. To see what—if anything—such a motoring activity might uncover spiritually. I lit a cigarette, hit play on 'Here I Am, Lord,' a hymn I've been digesting for the past couple of days, and off I cruised with no firm destination in mind but open to the possibilities of the road ahead.

Normally, when I decide to entertain these sun or moon-chasing drives, I ease into them by just kind of rambling along the way in fourth gear. Absorbing music and cleansing the build-up of shite in my head. Usually, but not always, I arrive at a destination, a dreamy patch of land called Someplace Else. A time and place a million miles distant from the road ahead or the one behind. Where images, aromas, sounds, and emotions converge for a few minutes—past, present, and future. It is here where truth sometimes surfaces. Finding the fortitude to face it is another matter, though.

As I was heading out towards the southerly roundabout of Tuam for the open roads of the M17 motorway, a panicked thought struck me.

'I'm spending too much driving time on motorways.'

A sudden sense that I might be drifting subliminally into cruise control on the perfect tarmac—and that revelations weren't to be found on auto-pilot, especially on this day. Automatic driving might lead to familiar, automatic thinking and so Someplace Else might not be found so easily. Or worse, might be a carbon copy of a previous blueprint but not thoroughly authentic. A question emerged from the grey mists of my mind.

In terms of my offbeat spirit investigation, are motorways akin to a form of artificial-intelligence danger to my soul-exploration?

I reached no satisfactory answer, but decided to invest thinking time on the subject during some milky-streaked night of the future. Anyway, newly superstitious, I manoeuvred a full-circle turn on the roundabout and headed back to town. There was only one obvious solution open to me. The narrow-framed, wiggledy-hipped N83 and its samba beat of countryside twists and turns.

The road is a national secondary route that government spending has mercifully forgotten to dump truckloads of cash on. It encourages alertness and risky overtaking manoeuvres. Nevertheless, it's a drive with lots of options, and easy access to many forgotten towns and wild villages of old. I opted for the delights of Dunmore, Cloonfad, and Ballyhaunis to kick off the afternoon's spirit proceedings.

The fields and hedges whizzed by as I listened to my solitary hymn on repeat. I slipped through a couple of villages that seemed to be rotting from the centre out. Once handsome places lined with sturdy old buildings, but now hollowed of soul and energetic life force. The cracked concrete hinted at a rich past, but the derelict buildings sighed with sadness and only faint echoes of better times remained—a haunting reminder that the reckless glory of Irish market towns will never return.

After about forty minutes, I pulled into a petrol station in Ballyhaunis to grab a cup of tea and rooted around the passenger seat looking for some spare change to pay for it. In my haste, I flicked a couple of two-euro coins onto the passenger-side floor and stretched over to pick them up.

As an aside, the tidiness of my mind can be accurately recorded by the state of Brigid's interior. On Sunday's audit, besides the obligatory half-box of L&M Blues, empty coffee cups, lighters, books, and some accumulated fan-mail from the Revenue Commissioners and Courts Service of Ireland—I unearthed a couple of odd socks, two jumpers, more loose change, leaflets, and a towel. Some decluttering and hoovering was in order and long overdue.

As I began the exercise by gathering up the loose change, I glanced up to the heavens, and the sun flicked a ray of approval in my direction before resuming its battle for air supremacy. A little later, in the shop, and after sticking two Barry's teabags into a cup and filling her up with hot water, milk, and a couple of sachets of sugar, a news notification from some mainstream newspaper popped up on my phone. The item—a prominent politician announcing he was recently 'diagnosed' with ADHD.

Hmmmm, I thought.

As someone in probable possession of an extra-strong mug of ADHD, the use of the word 'diagnosed' triggered a negative emotion. Diagnosis implies disease. Now, if it is an actual set of coherent and labelable things, ought it be treated not primarily as a mental health disorder, per se, but rather a gift.

A divine one.

Many types of people experience the world differently. Men and women with Down Syndrome, for example. In general terms, many people might be tempted to view a world with less Down Syndrome as a good thing. People with it have a much lower life expectancy, although it has risen hugely in recent times. However, along with all of the worry, heartache, and health issues that undoubtedly come along with Down Syndrome, especially for parents and siblings, it also comes with something else.

Down Syndrome births pure love into the world.

Consistent innocence and anam-croí flow into a world where the shelves of both are running emptier and emptier. So, the way I frame looking at this overall picture is to ask a question.

What price does the world pay spiritually for the absence or denial of this type of love and innocence gifted to it?

Unfortunately, the priorities of Lego-town existence seems to dictate a requirement for mankind to process the world in an identical manner. A more controllable, predictable earth is the desired outcome. Or, to use that dreaded marketing term of the recent past—a safer and more effective one.

An ADHD life is a life filled with endless streams of questions and sparking ideas, if not so many solid answers. I can't imagine a life without these questions or one especially enhanced by automatically reaching for a pharmaceutical intervention to 'fix' me. In short, medication is not worth the sacrifice of so many of my questions.

But that is just plain old bonkers me. Each to their own.

The word 'diagnosed' subliminally suggests not just disease, but that there is something wrong with the person. Once my mind latches onto a problematic issue like this in a sentence, it's off to the races we go.

Diagnosed—scientific-word—prescription-medication—pharmacies—bookies—every-town-has-lots-of-what—pharmacies-and-bookmakers—Addictions-and-prescriptions—prescriptive-society—get-them-addicted-to-something—prescribed-to-something—control—control—control—Hmm—maybe.

A lot of maybes, but after considering the news notification on my phone as above I didn't come to any answers, instead the old natural computer spits out two questions.

How much medication is my town on?

How much medication are the politicians on?

Right around the appearance of these new questions, a beam or two of sunshine shot through the cloud cover again and blinded my overthinking. Soon, I exited the petrol station and followed a signpost pointing Brigid in the direction of the holy town of Knock. A place I seldom go.

The interior of Knock Basilica is nothing like I remember it from my youth. I've visited the smaller church located on the same grounds a number of times over the years, but was never an avid fan of the concrete monstrosity erected in the mid-seventies in preparation for the papal visit of 1979. The exterior still looks much the same, but I must admit the interior is quite a different spectacle altogether nowadays. Surprisingly so. Modern yet tasteful. Vast, airy, and very high-ceilinged with the feel of an auditorium.

The altar is strategically placed in the centre, with the sectioned-off pews circled around it. It was quiet, so I walked around at a leisurely, touristy pace. Stopping here and there to read some of the history and also to brush up on the reason why Knock holds a special place on the Catholic Church's holy sites map—because of the apparition of Our Lady, Mother of God.

At a rough estimate, I reckon there is comfortable seating for about 1,200 people inside the basilica. Any music or choir must sound unreal and otherworldly in this huge, open space. A magnificent wall mural depicting the apparition of Our Lady in Knock dominates the eyeline regardless of where you sit or stand. It is spectacular to behold, to be fair.

The apparition story began on the 21st of August 1879, when fifteen people from the village of Knock witnessed an apparition of Mary on the gable wall of the parish church. They said she appeared with St Joseph, St John the Evangelist, a lamb, an altar, and a cross. The small congregation huddled together and watched this sight in the pouring rain for two hours, reciting the Rosary.

I plonked down on a seat at the back of the empty basilica and tried out a decade of the Rosary for size. Counting Hail Marys in one's mind is a particular nuisance for the ADHD-inclined, as the brain tends to wander off the abacus quite easily. I stopped the Hail Mary routine after I arrived at a sufficient passage time where I adjudged that the number of Hail Marys recited must surely have been safely above ten and probably closer to twenty. At any rate, a suitably weighty number in case any independent adjudicating angels were floating about the place taking count on clipboards.

After I ceased praying, I began focusing on the massive wall mural. I found a pocket of peace just gazing at it. My mind began slowing down and soon the engine spluttered to a halt. Some people refer to this as meditation, I suppose. Soon, I was in danger of falling fast asleep until my eyes dropped momentarily to the floor and noticed there were no knee rests in the pews on which to kneel. My brain was immediately activated by this anomaly, and was off again. But, eventually, I set aside further thoughts on the glorious mystery of the missing knee-rests and managed to let it all go. Although it's important to get the technical details of the basilica right, I would argue. I don't live a detail-orientated life, but I notice details keenly. Often, insignificant details are the windows to a world of truth about people, places, and things.

After a time, I got up, stretched the legs, and went looking for my county outside. Yes, you read that right. A roofed walkway encircles the Knock basilica with pillars placed on the outer side at equidistant points, and these pillars hold up the roof covering. Each concrete column is dedicated to a county in Ireland and is built with stone from that county. I loved this county idea as a child and we always ran around to find ours on school or family visits. I find I love the idea as an adult just the same. Soon, I found the mighty county of Galway and its handsome pillar of stone.

Thoughts about the ancient apparition got me to thinking about the world we live in. Many of the current happenings in this world seem apparition-like in nature. To me, at any rate. That I am, in a sense, standing at that old parish gable looking up at a world that scarcely seems credible yet is as real as real can be. But what stares back from the stone isn't Mary, Joseph, or John the Evangelist.

Rather, it's most of the world. I often—unimaginatively—use the term 'Lego-town' to describe the systematic foulness of what has consumed the globe. However, it strikes me that being aware of Lego-town, and its evils, doesn't make me a special category of person. Merely pointing it out and being aware of it doesn't save anyone from its clutches. I'm still in it, and like most have no definitive strategy to escape its ensnaring vine ropes. This raises another question.

Can anyone truly leave it, I wonder?

To be frank, I am not confident, but my survival instinct is whispering to me, at all times, to keep trying. I don't know why I feel this way. When those fifteen pilgrims gathered together a century and a half ago for two hours in the wind and the rain with their faith, rosary beads, and poverty, I assume not all in Knock observed the vision on the gable wall that they did. We all have to find our own apparition of truth and carve out a path, I guess, and have faith it leads eventually to the same place. A good place.

Was it a real apparition of Our Lady and the divine in Knock in 1879?

I can't know. But I believe that those fifteen people believed. And their simple faith is more than good enough for the likes of me. A peaceful thought and relaxing truth to chew on. In the meantime, I'll try to keep off the lures of motorway spirituality and stick to the byroads as often as possible. In case, one day soon, I forget, forever, to even attempt these journeys into the wilderness of myself.

Now, that follow-on thought does not especially please me to write. As it is, at times, kind of hellish to break away from the comfortable so often. This year is marked by elections, both here and abroad. The aroma of hope fragrances the air. Yet my urge to strike away from emerging groups and heroes pulses faster. Because they all, as far as I can observe, are content to self-contain safely within the overall Lego-town algorithm. I've dipped into the political coverage, like everyone else, and probably won't resist the lure of dropping back into writing about it again in the future. However, a thought crystallised in my head yesterday as I walked away from Knock shrine and back to Brigid. I can't fix or break out of Lego-town by habitually engaging with the false but alluring promises of it. The algorithms have already figured that part out and no doubt have made the necessary adjustments. A remorseless and endlessly self-preserving mathematical formula.

The alternative?

Well, I guess, to live like a boreen bandit armed with a couple of prayers and the odd hymn singing in my heart. Dipping into the strange new world but mostly out. With new visions to chase and old ghosts to face.

The spring is just around the next hedgerowed turn in the road. New words will soon bud and blossom on the thorny sleeves of the whitethorn bushes. A highwayman, perhaps, living as far from the maddening highway as possible. Faithful that the sun does eventually blast through the clouds at the moments you least expect it to, breathtaking in its raw beauty, power, and divinity.

Vaccinating the Blood of Jesus Christ

A few minutes ago, on a little fag break from procrastination, I could see a sky outside that is black and clear and bejewelled with diamonds. But, I'm back lying on the couch now—ageing away—and wondering on matters great and small. Again. Alongside me is my semi-faithful Jack Russell who is dozing and resignedly accepting the autumn of her life with a touch more grace than I.

She's fifteen and I've noticed it takes her a few attempts to hop up onto the couch beside me in recent months. Not as sprightly as even a year ago. Similar to me, I suppose. She seems stiller than her distracted tiller, tonight, though. Two spirits beached on a sofa engulfed by a sea of my inner dialogue.

On Good Friday, I drove to Galway Cathedral to take a knee and offer up some prayers to Himself. I got waylaid and made a detour to meet someone for a coffee. So, I arrived later than planned and as a result walked slap bang into the middle of the Good Friday service. It had not been my intention to attend the service but merely to rattle off a quick decade of the Rosary and light some candles.

But, what's meant for you won't pass you by, as they say.

As I took my position on a pew near the back, I noticed the Bishop of Galway was in attendance. A timely reminder that Good Friday is a bit like an All-Ireland final Sunday for the Catholic Church. The crucifixion of Jesus was playing out on the altar.

Within a few minutes, the crucifixion reading was at an end and the main celebrant of the service moved from the altar to the pulpit to deliver his sermon. Easter this year fell on the same weekend the clocks jumped forward an hour into summertime, but the priest's sermon seemed intent on setting the clock back to our darkest winter. Back to pandemic times, and for some reason he began tuning the spirituality fork of his congregation into vaccinations and the pandemic era. Vaccinations and immunisations, to be precise.

A weird analogy emerged. The priest compared a vaccine—the injection of a virus to stimulate an immune response—to how the metaphorical blood of Christ might be considered to work in the bodies of the faithful. I can't say for certain how the sermon ended, though. Because I had an immediate immune response to the words coming out of his mouth. Quite literally, I spontaneously sprang out of my seat and left the packed cathedral. As fast as my shoe leather could carry me. The episode hit home hard and it's taken me a while to figure out exactly why.

The pillars of our society, whether church or state, never properly atone for their coercions. Ever. Never do they fully confess to their promoted sins. If they atone at all, that is. Instead, they seem to covertly advertise them. Whether it be the Pandora's vaccine box era of the Irish state, or the child abuse era of the church. Can these twin pillars ever rise from the rubble while they're permitted to get away with skipping the confessional box so often, I wonder.

Emboldened, they'll vaccinate the blood of Jesus, straight from the preacher's podium, to make a point or whitewash a transgression—if that is the course of action required. I wonder what Jesus would think listening to His blood be compared to a pharmaceutical product. I'm not sure how many Masses are in my future with sermons kicking off like this one. A rage I thought had died quite a while ago still burns a little inside me on this subject, I guess. The embers not quite white-hot but smouldering nonetheless. Catholic Mass might be more tolerable without the intervention of modern-day sermons and secular ideologies.

A few hours after my cathedral escape, I drove ninety minutes to Lough Nafooey high up in the Partry Hills. I guess I still needed a little more spiritual connection for the day that was in it. It was my fourth appearance at this spot in the last week or so. Searching for something within without quite hitting the bullseye.

On the way, I listened to some music and conjured up a short protection prayer. Then recited it a few times in my head until I was happy with the results and certain I would remember it in future. An uncertain man stepping through uncertain territory. On the edge of the lake, I asked for guidance and offered what little I had within me in return. A prayer to the lapping waters, mountains, stars and Himself. I felt a little of His presence and truth blowing through the wind and watering my eyes. A light sparked. So, I turned and muttered. Then, cursed and barked. Saddled with renewed hope, I drove away.

Reminiscing about this whole episode generates enough energy to lift me off the couch. I move outside to smoke another cigarette and think. White, puffy clouds move low and visible across the dark sky now. Nonchalantly and without a care in the world. Another glimpse of the beauty in nature.

Where is my spirit within supposed to be consistently regenerated, I ponder. These men of the cloth are too often inconsistent and unbrave and getting in the way. Not bad men, per se, but what kind are they exactly?

I don't have answers, only questions. I'm not even certain I understand the questions I need to explore half the time. But, there was a truth in my reaction to the sermon and one which I can't seem to ignore. Indeed, increasingly I feel it's dangerous to my spirit to ignore it. Ultimately, that's the fucking problem, isn't it?

Hmmmm.

Interlude: My Favourite Word

My favourite word is 'beautiful.'

I can think of no other that even comes close; it has many synonyms but no substitute. Not really. Not for me, anyway.

Often, I listen to people carelessly and casually utter the word, or pen the letters neatly in a digital post or comment—failing to properly attune to its radiance, I feel. Myself included, sometimes.

Beautiful is not a word constructed of the mind, but rather one with beginnings deep within the womb of the soul. An expression to be absorbed and immersed in.

Each 'beautiful' gestates and journeys, struggles and fights, for its unique life and light. Fighting for a little notice in the unnoticing world. An inner word pulsing out from dark pools, brave and true. Too many stop only to notice her finished product and miss the battle every 'beautiful' has fought for that beauty.

Only the chosen few can attain stunning attractiveness—but all have access to a little beautiful, I think.

Today, the sun shone high and mighty over the west coast of Ireland. A gorgeous day. A fine afternoon for observing beauty and the beautiful pulsing out of nature's deep core. And for feeling the throb of these letters from farmyard beasts and vibrating across seaside puddles. Seeping out of piebald ponies and some of the piebald people too.

God, no amount of sun cream could keep the beautiful at bay today.

Life on the Road Less Travelled

The first thing I noticed was the thin films of clean, brown earth compressed beneath Lugh's fingernails. His grip was strong and the backs of his hands were tanned from soil work and the ever-changing microclimates gusting onto the mountain slopes of North Connemara. A reward for a life spent outdoors. You don't see hands like that anymore, I thought to myself.

I glanced over at Pomona; she too possessed amazing hands. Long-fingered like Lugh's, strong digits but thinner and retaining their femininity. I could imagine Pomona treating herself to a little classical piano with them after digging a couple of rows of potatoes from the back garden. Both were healthy and hardy thin. I must confess, though, I spent the first thirty minutes in their company slightly mesmerised by the nimbleness and expressiveness of their fingers. Their hands seemed to speak a language all of their own.

A book by Walter Macken lay face down on the kitchen table along with some tobacco pouches for rolling cigarettes and other non-eating bits and bobs. This, along with the wear of the table, seemed to indicate conversation and contemplation held forth on this square yard of wood as much as food. Pomona casually shared with me that she was reading a Wim Hof tome. I imagined the table held meals, intelligent chatter and the exchange of ideas and opinions—comfortable silences and the odd heated row too. Intellectuals of the land and of the hand. I am a good judge of a kitchen table, usually.

We eased into the verbal exchanges, exploring the ideas and learnings to be garnered from the books they were reading. They rolled tobacco and I smoked from my manufactured packet. Pomona brewed tea without milk and served it with a little brown sugar. It tasted delicious. The beige-coloured Stanley range fire was an arm's length from the table and heated the room with turfy and woody goodness. They used the range oven to cook meals but also to dry fruits and some vegetables from the garden.

Soon, they told me a story about a pear from the pantry.

One evening, Lugh put a pear on the hot plate and left it on top of the range to warm. Lugh being Lugh, he quickly forgot about it and soon the piece of fruit started to sizzle. As the heat from the hot plate increased, the underside of the pear began to turn to juice just beneath its skin. The natural chemical reaction made the pear spin rapidly around the plate in ever-quickening circles.

At this point, Pomona excitedly jumped into the storytelling to relay how both watched in amazement at this tiny bit of natural magic—and of how it made them laugh. They looked at each other in innocent joy as they recounted the details of the spinning, sizzling pear and of how the sight of it took their breaths away. I tried to remember when such a simple discovery gave me comparable pleasure. So long ago—I couldn't think of one. I envied them a little for their uncomplicated joy and loved that people like this still existed in the world. I was certain in that moment that I needed to fill my life up with more of them.

Later, Pomona spoke again and there was emotion in her eyes. I detected traces of recent sadness in her voice too. She was still healing from a family bereavement, she confessed. Also, there was a continuing disconnect between Pomona and her family over the life she had chosen to live. Not many understand the life lived on the road less travelled, halfway up the lower slopes of the Partry Mountains, I suppose. She still tried to remain bright and cheerful in speech, though.

Lugh was a good match for her, I thought. He was a good fifteen years older and had lived a different life before meeting Pomona a dozen years previously. I sensed he had negotiated some of the same familial obstacles she was dealing with now and understood them. Her family's opinion of him didn't seem to bother him in the least.

I liked that about him.

Pomona's mind and words move quickly when she is excited by a topic of conversation—similar to me in that regard. Lugh, though, was different. When Pomona or I completed a spoken piece of thought, Lugh paused a couple of heartbeats before making his point or interjecting his thoughts into the conversation. This was to ensure the speaker was completely finished talking. A mark of respect and patience. I liked that they both quoted each other's words. An observation or an insightful comment Lugh might have uttered in the past would be referenced by Pomona in something she was saying in the present and vice versa. It revealed the high value they held of the other's opinion.

My tour of the gardens started in the bathroom with the compost toilet. Everything in the house seemed to have multiple functions. The pee and poo had separate exits from the house and separate functions in their composting science. Everything and everyone had chores to do, in other words—most especially the worms at the bottom of the toilet bucket.

Lugh spoke with the same warmth and wonder about worms as W.B. Yeats once penned poems about Maud Gonne. He carefully brought me through the whole composting routine. The human waste went through one routine and the food waste went through another. Central to it all was the function of the worms to break down biological matter naturally. In one composting bin I noticed some cardboard and I enquired about its purpose—about whether it would decompose into compost.

'Oh, the worms love cardboard, sure just look at this…'

Lugh then pulled back a piece of cardboard and flipped it over. Families of worms were nesting in it—busily and methodically breaking down the material while also taking time to procreate like maniacs during assigned cigarette breaks from the worms' union. I was dumbstruck and fascinated by it all.

The gardens themselves were a wonder of creativity and different species of fruits, berries and vegetables. Cherry, plum and apple trees. Blackberry, raspberry and gooseberry bushes. Cabbages, broccoli, potatoes, herbs, rhubarb and a dozen other delicacies growing whose names I didn't recognise, nor can I remember now.

Pomona came alive in the garden. As she spoke, she couldn't resist kneeling down to tend a flowerbed here or pull some weeds there. She checked on an experiment she was trying out on a rhubarb plant that involved what looked like a chimney pot and lid. She let out a squeal of delight when she found that her new idea was working. When she removed the lid it revealed that the rhubarb stalk and leaves beneath were now towering above all the other rhubarb growing around it in the earthy bed. Both explained the importance of rotating the crops and not planting root vegetables in the same beds of clay year after year. Pomona kept detailed charts and notes about the composition of the garden.

The planting season for many vegetables had just begun, and I was amazed to see that some of the planted seedlings and vegetables were covered in woollen sheep fleeces provided by a local sheep farmer. The fleece provided a protective layer from spring frost over newly seeded beds. Lugh brought me across a small mountain stream to another field where many of the fruit trees were located. Though the trees were still bare, I noticed a layer of something packed around their bases.

Seaweed.

'Seaweed is great for feeding the trees,' he whispered confidentially.

Later, Pomona unhappily recounted the story of a Canadian company that had bought up the rights to Irish seaweed along the Galway and Connemara coastline. I had no idea that seaweed was such a valuable fertilising resource, or indeed, that it was something our governing forces could sell off the rights to for thirty pieces of silver. Yet another slice of our ancient land hoovered up by a faceless company for profit, right under our noses. I decided not to let the news ruin my visit, though.

I marvelled at the ingenuity of the couple. The harshness of the Connemara landscape is such that even on three acres of land, the composition of the soil can change from bog to rock very quickly. They knew every inch of their soil and what lay beneath it. Pomona was again experimenting with growing spelt and rye on a small mound of soil adjacent to the cottage. In the year ahead, she wanted to take the process of bread-making right from seed to oven.

After the garden tour, they insisted I stay to break evening bread with them and Pomona produced a steaming vegetable curry from the oven, bubbling with enticing aromas plucked from the gardens. I hadn't even noticed she'd been cooking, so engrossed was I with their stories, work and fruits of their garden labour.

Over dinner, they spoke of living in community with the wildlife—happily existing in the presence of the birds, bees and the odd dragonfly too. The birds strutted amongst them nonchalantly in the garden and Pomona revealed how they communicated with each other, and of how they flirted with one another too.

One night, Lugh and Pomona were out for a walk on the road by Lough Nafooey when they were met by a cauldron of bats. The bats swooped down in formation and flew directly towards the couple. Then at the last moment, a couple of yards away from their path and their heads, the bats abruptly changed course and shot up vertically like an arrow.

Straight up.

The bats were putting on a performance for Lugh and Pomona. They circled round and repeated the same manoeuvre five or six times in a row as the couple strolled along by the lake. There was no question that the two would be fearful of such an occurrence—merely, appreciative wonder.

'And sure, bats are hoors for showing off anyway,' Pomona helpfully added.

Before I bid them farewell, I heard Pomona let out a screech of happiness from a room off to the side of the kitchen.

'Look at the sunset over Lough Nafooey!'

Both Lugh and I got up from the kitchen table and wandered into the small sitting room. It was a sight to behold. So pleasantly distracted had I been by the whole visit, I'd barely registered the view of Lough Nafooey and the mountains that were within their possession from the small cottage and three-acre site.

'I was passing the road outside on a motorbike in 1997 and that's the view that made me buy this place all those years ago,' Lugh said.

We gathered around the window and watched the sun peacefully dip below a mountain above the lake for a minute or two. As it disappeared, I felt the moment had arrived to leave them be and return to a world much more travelled in. I was a little sad to go and a part of me yearned for my own three acres of heaven.

I left with gifts of rhubarb, dried fruit, broccoli and a jar of raspberry jam—grown by people who had loved them. As I ambled out to the gate, laden with these gifts, a thought occurred to me and I mulled over it as I started my car and pulled away.

Some people speak with their voices and some people speak with their words. But a few special people still speak with their earthy and soil-covered hands.

A Stained-glass Window

An under-publicised and poorly researched feature of St. Bridget in the books, Celtic mythology and Christian journals relates to the largely unknown fact that one of her current manifestations in the world is in the material form of a Peugeot 306 in the West of Ireland. Bet many of you scholars didn't know that.

Having been gifted her company for close to a year and cruising around the island with her, I can say with no little surety that she possesses both Christian and pre-Christian vibes. Saintly, for sure, but with an unusual and divine ability to coax out a little sun to pierce through downpours of doubt and who dims the headlights if religiosity teeters on the brink of dogma.

I must admit, I have a growing fascination with the era of Irish history where the spirituality of pre-Christian Ireland and Christian Ireland must have co-existed together for a time. Hundreds of years, possibly. This period seems like a fallen bridge of opportunity in my mind and spirit. A lost wisdom of history and inner-knowing no longer easily accessible to us as a nation.

This sense is a difficult feeling to enunciate, and one, perhaps, requiring the assistance of Brigid and our travels together to flesh out a little. Christian West of Ireland seems like the busy Galway to Castlebar road with its modern vehicles and changing traffic patterns. A road that with a few additional twists and turns will eventually lead you to Croagh Patrick, Ireland's holy mountain. While pagan Ireland or pre-Christian Ireland is a destination a few miles to the left of the main road, sited in the waters and deserted islands of Lough Corrib. More elemental in nature yet reassuringly unchanged and still. Less inclined to bend to the whims of man or time. It also has some roots and secret passageways that lead to the same holy mountain.

The two worlds are close but so very far away from one another too. Yet, it's when I'm excavating down the winding byroads that I find most of my windows of contentment and brief moments of inner enlightenment. Recently, I was watching a couple of videos on some ancient order of Irish druids or other, when the narrator referenced a famous stained-glass window dedicated to St. Bridget. It's a glass mural located in St. Mary of the Rosary Catholic Church in Cong, County Mayo.

Hmmmm, I thought.

I go to three churches to pray, with none of them particularly close to me, but St. Mary's is the one I visit most often. The chapel is close to the natural elements of Ashford Wood, you see. I normally drop into the church and then go for a walk in the forest. A bit of yin and yang, probably. Now, I was mildly annoyed I had never noticed the stained-glass window dedicated to St. Bridget referenced in the video on one of my many trips there over the last year or so. A simple reed St. Bridget's cross on one of the church walls is what keeps drawing me back to St. Mary's as much as anything else.

So, armed with my new information provided courtesy of a pagan rabbit-hole, I returned once more to Cong and Christianity to try to discover Bridget again. Behind the altar I studied the series of stained-glass windows with a closer eye. And, lo and behold, quite close to a stained-glass of St. Patrick there she seemingly was.

St. Bridget.

I smiled and after gazing fondly at her multi-coloured panes for a while moved towards my normal seat in front of the wall which held the reed cross of her. But when I glanced up to the wall, I observed that the cross was now vanished. As in gone. Unfortunately, a lad traipsing down briar-blocked by-roads between lakes and motorways takes meaning from these minuscule details, rightly or wrongly. So, instead of too much praying on this day, I lit a candle for all of the people currently residing in my heart and left to seek her out in the woods.

I suppose that's the thing with Brigid. Always on the goddess move yet usually staring straight into your face from a stained-glass window.

PART 3: SHADOWLANDS

A Fork in the Road

Looking back, I can see three significant periods of deep introspection over the last few years. I've never considered them bouts of depression, although many of the outward symptoms were the same. Lengthy arm-wrestles with my unhealed aspects a more apt description. In recent times, my forays into the wilderness with Brigid seem like acts of restlessness and nervous energy more than exhaustive journeys inching towards truth. We run into sheets of fog and driving rain a lot. I can't ignore a salient fact about these visits to the shadowlands. Two of the trips have occurred in the last few months, almost back-to-back.

Indeed, the most significant one of all has just ended, and it was extremely painful to process. My life ahead, and its meaning, are central to the internal wrangling and to the impact these choices have on others. It was doubly painful because I'm a slow learner, or, more accurately, I'm a slow decision-maker. I half-make decisions and then half-implement them. This eventually leads back to square one and a hell of a lot of unnecessary turbulence. Doubt and inertia cripple me at times in the same way slipping into overconfidence can, too.

A feeling has been humming within for a while that the year ahead is going to be, by far, the most significant of the last four or five years. I feel, at a deeper level, there are paths to choose that can no longer be ignored.

A fork in the road.

The past twelve months have felt like an attempt to walk in multiple realities at once. It is too exhausting to continue. It may mean saying goodbye to some people for a while or forever. It may also be time to bid adieu to political word-carving, at least by traditional methods. As far as I can ascertain, there are no satisfying solutions to be found in the Irish political realm as it exists at present.

Smartphone living serves up endless cycles of technological heroes and villains for daily consumption. This subtly triggers the psyche into certain lines of writing investigation and energetically saps my attention. Most political discourse is underwhelming, juvenile and designed with clickbait in mind. Ireland, like most western nations, seems to be running its government digitally on social media platforms. The essence of the nation is evaporating, as our attention is robbed by the glowing screen.

Many hoot and holler that the years ahead will be a spiritual war. I've probably uttered this phrase nonchalantly in recent conversations too, but I've only occasionally been cognisant of the actual depth of the words and what they feel and mean internally. A widespread concept seems to have developed that many who believe themselves to be on the correct side of some of the wackier political tyrannies of these times are also well-positioned in the correct army for the spiritual battles ahead. I wouldn't be so cocksure. Pointing out that something is true is not preparation for it.

All I can say for certain is that I struggle—daily—to make any gains on my spiritual battlefield, blazing away within, let alone anywhere else. And during this last cycle of self-examination, these dogfights were mostly night-long battles—an accumulation of inches forward and inches backward. I don't feel like a man making mile-long leaps into new spiritual dimensions.

An examination of the spirit must surely play out on an individual, internal level before anything can shift further downstream in any greater external spiritual war at play in the world. New political manifestations are further downstream from that again. Many, I'm sure, are winning this war a damn sight better than I am most days of the week. In my own case, I now understand that this will be an ongoing street brawl till my last breath on earth—any lingering doubt about that is now removed after the last couple of months.

I keep running around in circles on this point with regard to how to move in this strange emerging post-pandemic world. My fingers, though, have been itching to type me into a different direction. More soul-aligned, hopefully. It's fair to say I've been hesitant to make the necessary adjustments at this fork in the road. The feeling has been pulsing away within for a while now.

A constant riff running through my output is technology. Evolutionary cycles in its development mean it now acts as an anti-god. Accidentally addicting attention is one thing but purposely controlling our behaviour patterns is quite another—which is where I believe we are at. Every man, woman and—unfortunately—child faces an enticing, seductive offer from the controllers of Lego-town. It goes something like this:

'Sell us your attention and we'll thieve your spirit into the bargain, you'll hardly even notice we've taken possession of the pesky thing—and you.'

As someone who knows a thing or two about addiction, I think I understand that we lose our most valuable possessions almost unbeknownst to ourselves. Not just the earthly possessions, but the really important stuff. Dignity, self-respect, self-worth and self-love, too, until one day the low point is reached when the vital core and spirit are up for grabs for a couple of shillings or a second-hand iPhone. We live in times controlled by forces that beg, borrow and steal our spiritual essence. From what I observe, the dark forces in the spiritual war are winning handsomely without anyone taking particular notice. So the fightback must start from within each and every one of us. No small task, that.

The West has gradually sold its soul over the last couple of generations and we are all at fault to lesser and greater degrees. Sadly, there is no quick fix to getting it back until we start talking to each other about how and why we sold it and then, the hardest bit, challenging ourselves internally about what we are prepared to do to restore ourselves. A new government tomorrow won't change these facts, I reckon. There's but one writing and life path for me, and I need to move on to it while I still can.

I've tossed, turned and stalled long enough at this fork in the road.

Lead us not into Temptation

Anyway, last Friday, I found myself in the Church of the Assumption in Kinnegad. A beautiful chapel, but totally empty. As an aside, I'm thinking of starting all future articles like this one with the word 'Anyway' as a literary device. This is to forewarn readers that they are jumping into my thought stream—like climbing aboard a white-water raft bound for rapids, with 'Anyway' acting as a foghorn warning that they may soon be spluttering at the bottom of Niagara Falls—waterboarded, but probably still alive.

Now, back on point. I must confess my preferred way to find a Catholic church goes something like this: empty, high-ceilinged, visually intoxicating, padded knee-rests, and exposed wooden roof rafters if at all possible. Thankfully, the Church of the Assumption in Kinnegad ticked most of my boxes on this day.

I rambled in through the main entrance, turned left, and soon hit upon the local advertising stand. Information on St Thérèse of Lisieux was on prominent display, and I was reminded that I'm bumping into images and statues of her a lot lately in small towns and built-up areas, as they say. However, a poster grabbed my attention. As posters go, it was a good one too—advising readers to sprinkle in a little meditation between their five decades of the Rosary.

'Hmmm. I like this idea,' I thought aloud to no one in particular.

Now, I should state, front and centre, that the Rosary ain't exactly my favourite form of prayer or method of passing through Kinnegad. My caffeine-addicted brain likes it even less. Admittedly, the rosary is much easier to entertain in a group setting, but I'm rarely in a group of more than one. At any rate,

I'm more of a prayer-sprinting, candle-lighting black sheep than a five-joyful-mysteries, middle-distance-running kinda spiritual beast when it comes to these sorts of matters. But the meditation advice hooked me in a little, as my brain pathways were in need of some rest and recuperation. So, I decided to give it a shot for the day that was in it.

Before I proceed, I should note that in the not-so-distant past, I've had a rather significant episode with the Our Father. As in, I repeatedly couldn't remember a specific line of the prayer while reciting the Rosary. And the line yours truly kept skipping over and erasing from his memory?

'Lead us not into temptation.'

Now, when this episode occurred—repeatedly—I immediately took it as divine intervention from the main man *Himself*. I've probably spent a good three hundred kilometres of Brigid time—if not exactly meditating on the significance of this happening, then at least considering some of the possibilities and ramifications deeply. The truth, though, is that I understood precisely what it meant in those repeated moments when it was pointed out to me. Perhaps not in my conscious mind, but at a level that permeates my spirit and feelings—where one feels a truth rather than being able to prove it with the aid of a mathematical formula.

I bring it up on this day mostly to say that I now try to be a conscious reciter of the Our Father. Yet, my mind does like to wander, and wander, and wander some more. So, whenever I recite the Our Father in a Rosary setting, an internal dialogue often begins after the fourth or fifth Hail Mary:

'Did I say the Our Father right?'

'Did I forget the fucking 'Lead us not into temptation' bit again?'

'No idea, start again.'

As you can imagine, I just love the Rosary. My version now contains about sixty-five Hail Marys and twelve Our Fathers. Last Friday, as I knelt down to pray, I soon encountered another problem—one of a more mechanical nature. Each pillar in the church had a speaker strapped to it. The speaker closest to me was emitting a little noise, making it quite difficult to focus on the prayers and arduous to relax into any form of meditative practice between mysteries. Low-level static—the sonic equivalent of white noise from the TV, if you like—filled the empty space. In the quiet, unoccupied church, it became even more aggravating on my senses.

All the speakers were mounted high, and as I scanned each one on both sides leading up to the altar, I thought maybe I was just unlucky to be kneeling beside a faulty one. After two and a half initial decades of the Rosary, and in a highly un-Zen-like state, I got up from my pew and walked down the aisle. To my dismay, each speaker had the same hum and interference coming through. Every single one. Near the altar and over to the right stood a life-size statue of Jesus; I ambled over and plopped myself down on a bench beside him, then continued on with my prayers. He didn't look particularly sorry for my troubles.

Focusing on the hum helped, and I managed to tune out the noise for a few seconds at a time. My attempted meditations between decades of the Rosary helped, but the humming kept breaking through. I resigned myself to my fate and plodded on to the finish line. At the end, as I walked back to Brigid, it occurred to me that the problems of the Catholic Church—when boiled down to their essence—are a lot like that faulty sound system.

Too often, they interfere with people's connection to Himself. Sometimes, it's best to turn the volume down altogether, help people find *Him*, and then back away.

Somewhere Else

I've been feeling the need to put my back into a piece of writing for a while. But determining exactly what to ram my shoulder against has evaded me. Not a lengthy piece, but something with a touch of intense purity. More for me than anyone else.

So, I have been wandering out of Lego-town in search of something undiscovered within myself—sometimes in church-related settings and sometimes in nature. The world feels to me, more and more, like a city built of Lego pieces. Stepping into it for too long, or taking it seriously, seems faintly ridiculous. Dangerous even. Less often, I write about the goings-on in this fantasy city, and mustering lasting emotion for its characters escapes me. Anger bubbles and boils over here and there, but it lives only as long as the length of time I choose to absorb the lies.

Sure, I scribble down things functionally about some of the characters and narratives at play—and sometimes diligently—then hit the publish button. But more often than not, I sit back down somewhere else. I often ask myself why I bother entertaining this at all any more, and the best I can come up with is the hope someone might stumble upon my writing and use a piece of it as a map to find the Yellow Block Road out of Lego-town for themselves. To point out there is an exit from the fluorescent lights—possibly many—and, by extension, they can always come back into it if they so desire. With this in mind, people might then dare to muster a little courage to at least consider leaving the city limits once in a while for a look around and to consume reality in a different way for a day or two a month.

Or more.

These days, I am usually somewhere on a hill, in a forest, in my car, or elbow-leaning on the railings of a causeway leading out to an island. Silently somewhere is a good description of me in these places I ghost into in quiet joy, sad tears, and peaceful understanding of the laughable limitations of myself as a Lego-town man. Yet, I experience too the limitless possibilities that beat within me as someone other than mortar and plastic bricks. This other world is signposted with invisible paintwork and translucent lettering, hanging from the branch of a hidden forest tree, or the gentle sponge of a step on a bog's path, or even in the heavy beam of powerful sunlight from a setting sun, divinely framed by a gap in some bushes.

All whispering to me that true existence lies within a lightly, nightly misted village picture frame called Somewhere Else. Sometimes, I find villagers and meet fellow travellers on the road moving towards this place, but often I do not.

Of course, Himself shows up more often than He doesn't. For it is all Himself, really, isn't it, when you escape the digital distractions? He comes not to prod, cajole, guilt, or boast.

No. Never.

He appears just as a gentle reminder that there is no escaping Him. He often comes disarmed, with that kindly and knowing smile of His, to let me know that He knows all the ways and places I've tried to outrun and outfox Him. You might say I'm growing tired of my own unchanging reflection and mental resistance.

Meanwhile, back in Lego-town, the last month or so has been taken up with two separate cases involving Brigid vs the Irish State. Specifically, the Courts Service is attempting to remove my driving licence from my wallet and call a halt to my moonlight moseying through the West of Ireland—on the lookout for Somewhere Else.

Someday, I might write about this period of personal history in greater detail, but for now, suffice it to say, I have been the beneficiary of a couple of quite remarkable miracles that have kept me cruising between the ditches. I bring this up merely to highlight a feature of my life I am noticing more and more. Somewhere Else is where I most regularly encounter and surrender to the divine will—and reap its unexpected benefits. Actually, the only place where the divine world pours and flows into this one.

Although I occasionally write about this aspect of my life, I find it increasingly difficult to find the words. Spirituality and religious practice are such entrenched positions in the modern world—and are, quite often, business practices nowadays. I don't ever want to become either. I have my own practices, which I adapt frequently, and the sole reason I am comfortable with them is because they challenge and wrestle with me every single day of the week. They are demanding, whispering, and exciting too. As a result, I'm not who I was two years ago, I am not who I was one year ago, and I'm not even who I thought I was going to be three months ago.

I get enough confirmations when I'm traipsing down the right path and plenty of warning signals when I veer off course. I'm sure I have written words to that effect before, but it bears repeating—if only to myself—this is how spirituality feels to me and should feel. Entirely my own. I don't want anyone else's, and I'm sure they don't want to inhabit mine.

So, in these terms, the future is something to be prepared for and embraced, rather than a prediction game of ego-fulfilling prophecies in Lego-town. Something to think and reflect upon further during my next stumbling visit to Somewhere Else with Brigid—assuming my wallet still contains a driver's licence. Although maybe on one of these fair days or nights I might never come back, and cast it into the gently lapping waves on the far side of the moon and Mutton Island.

A Dream within a Dream

Outside the Realm

I've over-peopled the last two weeks. The more ancient I become, the more alone time I need—to mine sufficient words worthy of the light of day. I was in a conversation last week and just kind of gave up on it mid-sentence. This has happened before when I've been over-peopling. Aggravated by my train of unthought and embarrassed someone was having to listen to it. I needed a pack-of-cigarettes moment to myself.

A moment where the last words spoken are:

'Can I have 20 L&M Blues, please?' and then nothing but silence until the entire contents are drained and evaporated into the smoky heavens. A dozen hours to reflect on this journey of mine and whether I'm making progress or just wordlessly going mad.

Yesterday, I was mooching around Galway city early doors, soaking up the mid-October sunshine. Headphones on and sipping an overpriced latte. Strolling, yet unable to tap into the ease and relaxation this activity usually grants me access to. This town is always humming out a different tune, which is one of its main attractions. The unseasonably warm day was matched with an unreasonable number of tourists still knocking about the place for this time of year. Maybe it was the combination of both that was aggravating my senses. Surely tourists should be banned from Galway come the end of September?—to save the climate or some shit like that. Someone should really stand at the top of Shop Street with a clipboard and stop the passers-by:

'Oh, is it New York you're from?—isn't that lovely now. Ah shure, take this little flyer here, and you'll see there in paragraph two the exact directions of how to get the fuck out of the country as quickly as possible—bye now and slán abhaile!'

I bought a tuna roll in a Centra convenience store somewhere off Dominic Street and parked myself down in the Claddagh, far from the maddening tourist crowd. I sat on the concrete bank of the River Corrib, where the always turbulent waters make their final dash for the sea. However, not even this location brought respite. A passing seagull promptly fell in love with my tuna sandwich and, before long, a queue of them were sat on the riverbank wall beside me. Aggressive, dark-magician-looking fuckers between you, me, and the wall.

I broke off a piece of bread and lobbed it into the foam of the river to distract them. Soon, a dozen more seagulls swooped across from the Spanish Arch. Galway's only far-right scribe was in danger of getting outmanoeuvred and meeting a sad, watery end. Mere yards from the open sea. There's the makings of a proverb or sean-fhocal in there somewhere, if only I was fluent in Irish or English.

So, I lay back on the grass to save myself from imminent death and closed my eyes. The words Lough Nafooey flashed across the seven-stitch scar on the top of my skull—the mark of a childhood altercation with the corner of a block wall, and a breach in the forehead where all logic and normality leaks out, in a most thunderous fashion.

Hmmmm. Lough Nafooey, I imagined again—warming to the notion. Dedicating an afternoon to holding court with oneself in silence ought to occur in a place empty of people but full of the world's natural properties, should it not?

Would Brigid and half a diesel tank of holy water get me there and back, I wondered. Of course, they would, I wondered back.

An Edgar Allan Poe poem began playing in my ears again—'A Dream Within a Dream'—and it was settled. For Lough Nafooey is a dream and all life is but a dream within that dream.

Entering the Realm

As I popped over the final brow of the final hill, I met a bus filled with tourists moving in the opposite direction.

Please God, no, I prayed. Not here too.

A few minutes later I parked up on the side of the road and it was magnificently empty of vehicles. I grabbed my book, copybook, a new pen, and decided this was a spot and afternoon for rolled tobacco.

I stretched on the dense, thick sands of the glacial lake and quietly immersed myself in the magic of my new reality. Gloriously alone. A swim was called for to fully circuit-break the mind. I knew it would be cold and I wasn't exactly prepared for swimming—not having shorts or a towel—but improvised.

Fuck, was the water cold. I spent ten minutes or so coaxing myself in deeper and deeper before I suddenly dived in and fully submerged. I felt certain a significant test had been passed, although uncertain on the subject. My frozen roar echoed across the mountains. Then a second dive and finally a third. I floated on my back for a couple of minutes and, for the life of me, couldn't think of a single thing worth thinking about.

I towelled myself down with a T-shirt and lay back down once more. Refreshed. Closing my eyes, I began to observe slow thoughts emerging and unhurriedly passing by. I remembered my twenty-fourth birthday and trudging up the Ennistymon Road in Ennis. And without warning, feeling so old in that moment. A young man but one running out of time. A constant life theme. 'Time is running out. Do something.' I smiled fondly back to the old worrier trapped in his youthful bones from the road ahead. Twice the age but now half as old.

Before long, I fell asleep. When I woke, I thought of how easy it had been to fall into it and yet how hard I had been finding it to come by in recent months. Worrying about things and people and the road ahead, I suppose. The old worrier not quite dead. I yawned and glanced at my phone. Twenty minutes or so snoozing, I calculated, but it felt like peacefulness and nourishment of much longer duration. I sat up to have a think about things and the writing path ahead—the oncoming lights and shadows.

Which direction to go?

I fell into memories of 1993 and the crashed Fiat Tipo. The bonnet welded to a cattle trough in a field, wildly drunk and headed for PJ's Niteclub in Dunmore on the backroads—moments before the accident. And then, I recalled the scene a couple of days after the crash and the youthfully unheeded but wise words of the old council worker, Jack Hession, when handing over a filterless Woodbine to me on our morning tea break.

'Drinking's a mug's game for people like us, you know?'

He never said much, old Jack, but when he did, the words were usually worth the wait. Even if it took another twenty-five years to fully grasp them. He was a reformed alcoholic of the cold-turkey variety. No such trifles as AA for Jack. The hard road was the only path he understood and trusted. About five feet four inches in his stockinged feet and about the same measurement in width. Mostly muscle and blocks for hands. He knew where every single manhole cover in North Galway was located and had opened and been down most of them. I doubt one single person knows or cares where they all are now. The patron saint of burst water mains, stopcocks, and safety valves was old Jack. God rest him. My youthful arrogance didn't quite comprehend that great wisdom can often be found at the end of a shovel. There was a big price for the slow learning.

Unfortunately, not long after this the conversation in my head was interrupted by voices from outside of it. I opened my eyes and two families were strolling and laughing further down the beach. The spell was broken, the outer dream interrupted, and it was time to take my leave. I'd let go of a few things and remembered a few more. All told, not too bad. I took my jeans and jumper off the chicken-wired boundary fence and put them on. It was time to go back to the dream within the dream.

Ready, perhaps, for a few more people.

Grief

About a week ago, I had an explosion of grief. It roused me roughly, smacking the sleep from my frazzled pillow. I never knew grief lay buried in the pit of my stomach.

But it does.

Or it did.

Yes, grief. Old and new and ancient in parts.

I felt it water-cannon through my eyes, icy shivers goosebumped my skin. Heaving up from a darkened well, then gushing in rivers. I settled still, as still as I could, while flashing images of good times and good people blurred by.

The hurt of another donkey-kicks the gut more than your own, when the windowpane shatters and dreams splinter into a thousand shards. I am down there somewhere, shiny and sharp and cutting in places. This suffering is not of me—but on me.

Grief.

I guess it lurks in the shadows of my underbelly. Beneath the fast food and fast times sit old chimes and past crimes.

Grief woke me up to say its goodbyes.

Oh, how sad I was to see it cut ties.

The Lady of Lough Derravaragh

- a short story on an ancestral pain

Conn opened Brigid's rear left-hand door and deposited the carrier bag onto the back seat. The plastic bag contained a large Italian pizza box and two portions of chips tightly wrapped in paper. Once safely placed on the seat, he slammed shut the door and quickly skipped around the front of the vehicle and hopped into the driver's seat. The evening was bitter cold with a biting northerly breeze sweeping down Friar Street, one of the retail avenues close to the heart of Mullingar town. He picked up the phone resting on the passenger seat and swiped it open to read the message from Fionnuala again.

—Do you mind bringing some type of takeaway?

—Anything, pizza, burger, fish 'n' chips

—I haven't eaten for a couple of days

He shook his head and smiled to himself while pulling a couple of steaming chips from his coat pocket, which he quickly lobbed into their new home between his lips. They were hot and vinegary, and he rolled them gingerly around in his mouth until they cooled down a little to the touch of his tongue.

Typical Fionnuala, he thought.

He'd received her invitation to visit only hours earlier, a first communication from her by phone in over five years. She usually just appeared when he was in some kind of bother with his ancestors. On that earlier phone occasion, she was half-starved to death too—he seemed to recall. He began munching away on the chips and warmed his mind with memories of their last hastily convened rendezvous and adventure. He scrolled up a little on his phone to re-read her original text.

—Hi Conn, I'm doing some clearing work on a Lady chained to the bottom of a lake beside my house.

—If you wanted to pop along, it might be fun!

—Which lake?

Conn had responded immediately, skipping the niceties of a formal greeting.

—Lough Derravaragh

He closed his messages and typed the Eircode of her location into Google Maps. Twenty-seven minutes. He looked around the streets of the town and could see dense fog was starting to form. The foot traffic on the pavements was at a midpoint between very busy and eerily quiet. It was an hour after peak traffic on a normal working day. Christmas lighting still illuminated the streets, not yet removed. The people unwilling, perhaps, to fully release the festive mood for another day or two. Conn observed the number and variety of different faces passing his car. Some new to the town and some ancient to the land. All oblivious to the earth and water spirits occasionally gusting up and down the road in their midst. Strange times, strange people, he thought. Very strange, indeed.

He sat for a while contemplating the road ahead. Then, almost idly, he turned the key to the ignition. Brigid's engine immediately sprang to life, which simultaneously brought an end to the debates of his mind. The lightness, almost superficial inanity of her messaging confirmed only a couple of things. All Conn understood for certain was that Fionnuala was anxious about something and needed his help. She rarely asked for or needed assistance, and this worried him. Fionnuala was the younger of the two, but the much older soul.

Fionnuala and Conn were from the same soul tribe and soul friends, or anam chairde as the natives preferred, back when natives still spoke the mother tongue and when anam chairde had much less difficulty recognising one another. Theirs was not a romantic incarnation on this swing of the merry-go-round, which was just as well as previous spins had seen major aggravations, minor outrages and petty jealousies, ping-pong back and forth between the two. The consequences of which were no little pain, hurt and the occasional second-degree murder.

Conn bent his head to locate the switch for his fog lights; he suspected they were going to be needed tonight once he escaped the fluorescent lighting of the town and pointed his snout out the Castlepollard road. He glanced across at his phone again— Twenty-seven minutes, it still advised. The food would be cold by the time he reached her, but he also knew Fionnuala wouldn't notice.

Conn exited the last roundabout out of Mullingar and headed up the R394 towards Castlepollard. The fog was thick and swirling. Even with the fog lights he could barely see forty yards ahead of him on the road. Traffic was light, but every couple of minutes a pair of oncoming headlights would suddenly appear out of nowhere right in front of him, startling him unexpectedly. His mind wandered to the waters of Lough Derravaragh and the obvious link between the Lady of the Lake and the Children of Lir legend. The significance of which Fionnuala didn't seem to fully grasp from the earlier rapid-fire text exchange.

To be frank, Conn wasn't altogether sure he could prove a link, as the ancient Irish myth seemed unrelated to the broad-brush strokes painted by Fionnuala about the Lady in the Lake. But equally, he never noticed a coincidence he didn't fully trust either. Abruptly, Conn was jolted out of his thoughts by the appearance of another set of ghostly headlights and he quickly jerked the steering wheel to the left to avoid a sudden end to the evening's events.

After a few minutes, he judged that it was time to enter the other realm completely. The kingdom of faeries, mermaids, and spirits—both good and ill—wandering the lands around him. So, he reached forward to turn on the radio, and then leaned back again to nestle into his seat while waiting for the song to arrive. Soon, a green road sign with large white lettering flashed by him on the left: Castlepollard 5. And with it the sound of guitar playing began reverberating around the enclosed world of his car.

He was close.

Heavy mists began rushing by faster now. A bad-looking bend beckoned ahead. Conn's foot hit the accelerator, aiming for a gap between two old oak trees. He held his breath and felt his heart quicken. Finally, he loosened his grip on the steering wheel and trusted his eyes to close. The darkness was lit by the sound of a young Irishman singing. His gravelly voice gently pierced the night. The haunting air cleared the remaining road of fog and nature's obstacles and as Brigid mounted the ditch, Conn's doubts began to fade.

Fionnuala's grateful smile radiated around the small kitchen-cum-living room between bites, but she didn't speak until she'd wolfed down the second-to-last slice of pizza from the box. An open turf fire further warmed and lit the room. Conn drank in the surroundings while watching her eat. It was a makeshift apartment contained within a large dormer-style house on a large site, and he noted it was unusually clean for the free-spirited Fionnuala.

'I know, I know, I've been cleaning and scrubbing all day,' she replied to the unspoken observation, her hunger finally sated.

'Guess how much I'm paying for this place?'

But, before Conn could muster a reply and observe that she was avoiding an explanation as to why she summoned him on this night, Fionnuala answered her own question.

'Fourteen hundred a month and that's at a discount because the landlady totally loves me,' she announced, delightedly shocked by the price of her own words. Conn sigh-grinned to himself. Fionnuala was always absolutely certain the whole world was in love with her. Which, to be fair, many were—except for the intermittent appearances of malevolent deviants actively trying to scorch her soul from the face of the earth.

'Come on now, Finn, are you trying to tell me the dominion of faeries has fuckin' cost-of-living problems?' Conn retorted in disbelief but playing along with her distraction game.

'No, no, no… Sheila's not a faerie!—Although I must admit she has a great many gifts, gifts she is completely unaware of,' Fionnuala laughed, then clarified.

'The house isn't part of the otherworld, just the lands and obviously the lake.'

'What's going on here, Finn, what kind of trouble are you in this time?'

'I'm not in trouble!' she replied touchily. But rose from the small kitchen table and began pacing around the room, considering what to say next.

'Can't a girl just want to see a boy for pizza?' she finally smiled.

'Not usually, in my experience,' Conn said evenly enough. He glanced to his left and out the big bay window. A three-quarters-full moon was high in the sky and illuminated the fields at the back of Fionnuala's apartment. Small fields that rose gently upwards, delineated by a series of beautifully manicured waist-high hedgerows. Fionnuala watched him scanning the scene.

'I probably won't even need a torchlight tonight,' Fionnuala commented. She was finally swinging around to the point of their meeting, but Conn switched track again.

'How's the Black and Tan keeping these days?'

'Conn, you know full well Stuart is not a Black and Tan! He's Anglo-Irish aristocracy for goodness sake,' Fionnuala replied with a little heat and exasperation.

'Ah, point of information m'lady. There is no such fucking thing, not even the Donnybrook faerie queens would conceive of such a daft feckin' notion. Is Stuart part of tonight's expeditionary force?'

Stuart was Fionnuala's on-again, off-again love interest in the world of men and fixed-rate mortgages. Hailing from the landed gentry class and four hundred acres of prime agricultural land somewhere above in Meath. The landholding was the remnants of one of the old landlord estates and Fionnuala had shacked up with Stuart there for a time in an old gatehouse that guarded the entrance to the estate. Meanwhile, Stuart's mother and aunt resided in the big house. Neither mother nor spinster aunt were at all pleased with Stuart's apparent ongoing grá for Fionnuala.

'He bloody well is not part of anything. Stuart is past tense now, Conn. P-A-S-T Tense!'

The sparks from her fire indicated to Conn this was a recent past tense and probably not far distant from the actual present tense, and it explained a little more about his own presence on this night.

'What happened?'

'What happened!—I'll tell you what happened. He rings me the week before Christmas to say he couldn't see me on Christmas Day or St Stephen's Day. Never mind any thought or invitation to come visit him.'

Conn couldn't resist a little dig and poke around under her skin.

'Ah sure, I suppose he didn't want to be leaving Mumsie all alone in fifteen thousand square feet of luxury at Christmas. Understandable I suppose.'

'Mumsie, I'll tell you about Mumsie!—Do you know what I told him? I said, 'Dear Stuart, do you know what would be an altogether wonderful treat for Christmas? Why don't you put on those nice paisley coloured pyjamas Mumsie bought you last Christmas and trot up to the Big House and fuck Mumsie on Christmas Day and dear Auntie Evil on St Stephen's Day, because you won't be coming anywhere near me ever again,' and I hung up the phone.'

Conn needed to turn away from her and look out the bay window for fear the eruption of spontaneous laughter bellowing from the depths of his stomach might become visible to her. Fionnuala could be a total dichotomy. At the one time airy, light and esoterically mysterious and otherworldly, right up until the moment she hitched up her skirt and removed one of a selection of steak knives from her garter belt. Even tonight as she gobbled down the takeaway Conn had provided she poured two cups of raspberry herbal tea as an accompaniment. Her innate trust in the goodness of people was at once admirable and often dangerous.

'That's the Tans for you. Turn your back for a second and you get a bullet lodged between the shoulder blades.'

Conn decided to move the conversation on. Whatever Stuart's faults, he understood Fionnuala saw things in him that Conn had never seen, and had come to accept her abilities to discover these qualities in people were as real as her affection for the West Brit aristocrat.

'Fionnuala, why is there a Lady shackled to the bottom of Lough Derravaragh?'

Fionnuala eased down her pacing and the angry outburst evaporated from her eyes. She looked across at him sheepishly and scratched at her mane of dishevelled reddish-brown hair. She was of medium height and slim build and wore plain, dark tracksuit bottoms with a white lycra training top. She was not familiar with the world of brassieres or upmarket lingerie outlets and so her heavy breasts swung dangerously, with a mind of their own, when she was in the full heat of emotional battle moments earlier. Both an alluring and disconcerting sight for Conn to witness.

'Well, first of all, she isn't a lady exactly,' Fionnuala began.

'What is she then?'

'Well, she's a… she's a mermaid.'

Fionnuala sat down at the table across from Conn and proceeded to allow her little dam to burst. What followed was a stream-of-consciousness outpouring of information. She'd arrived near Derravaragh six months earlier, guided to the location by her spirit-guide with the express purpose of releasing the Lady of the Lake from a curse. A curse that left the mermaid chained to the bottom of the lough and guarding a portal to one of the other worlds. In typical Fionnuala style she left her work till the end of her stay, and was already set to move further north to Carrick-on-Shannon in a couple of weeks.

Fionnuala hinted that the curse might have been cast by a lover who'd developed a taste for Christianity. A man in layman's terms. Conn knew Fionnuala's distaste for organised religions and the like could, at times, cloud her judgement but remained silent. She was very much closer to the druidic practices of old.

In Irish mythology and literature, druids were often portrayed as powerful magicians with supernatural abilities, but a simpler interpretation, and one both Conn and Fionnuala identified with more, was druids acting as intermediaries between humans and the divine. Fionnuala observed Conn's preoccupation and connection, down through the ages, with moon, sun and water energies, often encouraging him to delve further into these druidic essences of himself. But he was more concerned with healing the patchwork quilt of spastics, as he labelled them, in his ancestral line in more recent eras. A tribe of pagans, priests, and heretics healthily slurry-spread with a flowing stream of rustic muck savages. Fionnuala thought he was overly hard on them all, at times. She noted they had some very special characteristics blended in with heavy trauma and only rudimentary coping mechanisms to deal with both the good and the bad. Not much different than most Irish ancestral lines stretching back through the annals of time. But Fionnuala admired that they stood at his shoulder cheering him on most of the time, a fact Conn rarely acknowledged.

The truth of Fionnuala's current situation was that she was confident she could deal with the impasse and obstacles in her way regarding the Lady of the Lake, but could admit privately to herself that Conn had a knack for recognising and dealing with some of the snarlier and gnarlier spirits roaming the lands. She also thought he was linked to this situation in some way but wasn't quite sure how or why.

'So, you've made three separate attempts to approach the lake and each time your spirit-guide has stopped you on the way?' Conn finally enquired after Fionnuala finished speaking.

'Yes, she keeps asking if I am clean enough and protected enough,' she offered in addition to the knowledge already shared.

'So, let me get this straight, your response to this question has been to bleach your apartment within an inch of its life and text your favourite pizza delivery driver,' Conn reacted, equal parts humoured and incredulous.

'Yes, exactly!'

'You do realise that Lough Derravaragh has been subject to an enchantment spell in its past?'

'You mean the Children of Lir. Of course, I know the story, but you can refresh me on some of the finer details, if you like?'

It never ceased to amaze Conn how little Fionnuala seemed to care about the actual recorded mythology and legends of the lands she roamed. Considering she floated amongst many of the subjects of these very same myths and legends at various times. So, he began a short, hurried account of the Children of Lir, a jewel in the crown of early Christianity but like many an olden tale needed the pizzazz of a little paganism to keep it alive, well and present in public consciousness. He began by pointedly noting The Children of Lir was one of Ireland's most famous legends, a tale of love, jealousy, and transformation.

'King Lír had four children with his beloved wife Aobh. However, after Aobh's untimely death, Lir married her sister Aoife to provide a mother for his children. Initially, Aoife loved her step-children, but grew jealous of their father's affection for them. So, in a fit of rage, cast a spell, transforming the children into swans. The enchantment condemned them to spend 300 years on Lough Derravaragh, 300 years on the Sea of Moyle and 300 years on the waters around Erris, in County Mayo'

Conn paused for breath, and, satisfied that Fionnuala was paying full attention, continued:

'On Lough Derravaragh, Lir stayed with his children, holding feasts and entertainments to ease their suffering. After 900 years, the children returned to their old home, finding it desolate and their father long dead. They then encountered St Mochaomhóg, a Christian missionary, who treated them kindly. When their enchantment finally ended, they transformed into withered old people. The saint baptized them before they peacefully died and were buried together.'

Fionnuala remained wordless for a couple of minutes after Conn's voice had faded away and then carefully began to respond. To herself as much as to the man sitting across from her.

'You know, Conn, in the wars of men they say the victors write the history. I wonder if in the spiritual realm the victors write the last two paragraphs of the myths.'

Conn decided not to start an argument with her on this point but instead said:

'So, we have a 900 year enchantment spell and a lady at the bottom of the same lake cursed. Might it not be a spell of some description?'

'You think pagans or faeries interfered with a mermaid? Are you completely and utterly mad, Conn?'

'I didn't say that, Fionnuala.'

'Then what are you saying?' she replied testily.

'I'm saying it's time to go find out.'

'So, you'll come with me?' she replied, her mood lifting a touch.

'Well, let me put it like this: I didn't drive through a bloody ditch just to drink your raspberry tea, Finn.'

A small, low wall marked the boundary between the site of the house and the picturesque fields behind it. At the centre of the wall was a small, iron gate and Fionnuala opened it and both of them trundled through.

'How long a walk is it?' Conn asked.

'Not long, maybe twenty-five minutes through the fields,' she answered.

The hill ahead sloped upwards, but it was a gentle incline and, after a few steps, Fionnuala linked arms with Conn. The three-quarters-full moon was even higher in the sky now and directly above them, and an evening that began foggy and windy was now completely still and crystal clear.

'I'm glad you're here,' she admitted and then gently bumped her head against his shoulder.

'I'm glad I'm here too,' Conn confessed.

The ground underfoot was pock-marked with cattle hooves and the grass was frosted a silvery white. It crunched beneath their feet, and so the music of their steps, along with the mist of their breath, transposed both of them into a quiet, almost meditative state. Conn reflected on what was ahead, but his mind ran back to his car and the last quick check he performed on his phone before departing Mullingar. A search involving Derravaragh and saints. Conn had no earthly idea why he chose such a random combination. The search returned one result.

St Cuarach.

A quick scan revealed St Cuarach was expelled from the monastery of Kells by St Columcille for breaching discipline. Conn immediately felt a warmth rising in his heart towards this far-away man. A renegade Christian, perhaps, Conn wistfully hoped. Cuarach then wandered the countryside until he reached Knockeyon, a hill on the south-eastern shore of Lough Derravaragh. It was passed down through the generations, by word of mouth, that Cuarach chose this remote location to live out the rest of his life in prayer and fasting. At some point, Cuarach became seriously ill and was near death. He prayed for water to quench his thirst, and miraculously heard water trickling from the rock above him. After drinking the water, he was cured. In gratitude, he built a small church dedicated to St Eyon somewhere halfway up Knockeyon hill, the ruins of which apparently still remained. As Conn reflected on the sourced information he couldn't help but wonder that water, water, water was linked everywhere in this little escapade of Fionnuala's.

Soon, the two of them reached the brow of the hill and paused to look downwards. Conn was expecting to see Lough Derravaragh but was surprised to note there was no view of the ancient lough at all.

'Where's the lake?'

'Oh, you can't see it from here; a thin line of trees guards the shoreline. We'll be nearly on top of it before the water comes into view. Actually, it was just before the treeline that spirit stopped me,' Fionnuala answered helpfully.

Fionnuala's words struck Conn as somehow relevant. She noticed the quizzical look in his eyes, furrowed brow and a mind beginning to churn as he scanned the fields and trees below.

'You know, the entire lake is surrounded by privately owned farmland, there's very little public access to Lough Derravaragh,' she added.

'Hmmm, interesting,' Conn murmured in reply.

They continued on, stepping down the hill of fields at a slightly improved pace. About halfway down, Fionnuala suddenly stopped and broke away from Conn's linked arm.

'Why don't we stop for a break, Conn?' she smiled, but there was a hint of trepidation in her eyes.

Conn pulled a small silver flask from his coat pocket; it was filled with ginger tea that Fionnuala had prepared just before they left the house. He twisted the cap open and then filled the cap and watched the steam of the orangey liquid reach for the heavens. He made to hand it to Fionnuala. She was gazing up at the stars and had a far-away look in her eyes. She turned slightly to him and accepted the cup.

'Spirit says hi.'

Conn looked at her and merely nodded. He didn't have any direct relationship with spirits or spirit-guides. He began reflecting on his vague awareness, at particular moments, of the collection of maniacs in his family-tree that he felt were with him but never said hello exactly.

'Spirit says they're not all maniacs.'

'Does spirit have anything useful to say about the Lady on the Lake?' Conn replied, changing the subject while trying to ignore the not ignorable fact of Fionnuala's spirit-guide casually invading his thoughts.

His enquiry was met with silence, and after a couple of minutes Conn glanced over at Fionnuala and could see she was kneeling while rummaging around in her jacket pocket for something. Then, she stood up and faced him.

'If we go ahead, we have to stay until it is finished and the curse is broken.'

Conn grasped the full seriousness of what this meant and bobbed his head up and down a couple of times in response.

'I suppose we'd better get cracking, then.'

Conn stood by a wire-mesh fence and then leaned against the last wooden stake planted in the ground right at the edge of the lake. The fence, he supposed, divided the different sets of farmland owners surrounding this patch of Lough Derravaragh. Fionnuala moved towards him with what looked like a translucent stone peeking out from her fist, which Conn assumed must have been the item she'd been searching for in her pocket earlier. She lightly clasped his wrist and placed the stone in the palm of his hand.

'And what do I do with this, Finn?' Conn asked, a little suspiciously.

Fionnuala looked momentarily at a loss for what to say next.

'J-just dip it in the waters and… do whatever comes into your head,' she half-stuttered, a little uncertainly.

'I can't tell you what to do or say, and I suspect it won't be what I'll do myself.'

Fionnuala moved away from him and sat down on a rock to remove her boots. Conn peered more closely at the stone in the moonlight and, although transparent and chilly looking, it felt smooth and inviting to his touch. He wrapped his fingers around it and felt the warmth and surprise of its power. It frightened him and excited him. He immediately thought of St Cuarach and couldn't think of anyone or anything else. So he slid away from the fence and placed a boot in the lake and then hunkered down. He slowly placed the tip of the stone into the water and held it there. It seemed to sparkle as it was hit by a ray of the three-quarters-full moon. He looked out across the waters and blessed himself with his free hand. He was suddenly nervous he might say or do the wrong thing.

'Cuarach, whatever roaming and malcontent spirits or dark spells have invaded these waters, please help Fionnuala to remove them.'

He whispered the words of prayer and nodded to himself, content that he had said exactly what he had wanted to say and the prayer came from his heart. He watched the barely dipped stone and saw small rings begin to circle in the waters around it, expanding, out and out, mesmerically into the lake. A rising, deep sadness seemed to pulse back and up through the stone, the force of which gripped Conn. For it seemed a dark sorrow very familiar and somehow personal to him. A teardrop fell and merged into the waters of the lake. Then, he simply rose and walked over to Fionnuala, who was now barefoot and ankle-deep in the water, and handed her the stone. He turned away to process his emotions and also hide them from Fionnuala.

Soon, he heard the low chanting of her voice intermingled with words and invocations. This was followed by a song in a language not English and not exactly recognisably Irish, but something older still. It felt strangely beautiful and possibly more ancient than Lough Derravaragh itself. The music of her voice seemed to balm the night air using the waters beneath her feet. When she finally stopped, Conn couldn't be sure how long they'd been there. He looked up at the moon and it seemed to have moved quite a distance.

'She's free,' Fionnuala said simply.

Conn grinned, delightedly.

'But she wants to know where she should go?'

Conn un-grinned, un-delighted.

'You mean neither of you knows?'

'Well, I can't be thinking of every tiny detail, besides she's a young spirit and a little flighty.'

'That makes two of ye then,' Conn replied shortly.

Conn's earlier sadness hadn't quite dissipated, so he didn't have the energy to get too upset about the situation.

'She wants to go to another lake or a river might do. Any ideas?'

Conn contemplated the question earnestly and thought about it.

'How about Lough Erne?' he offered.

Fionnuala swirled the stone ever so gently in the water.

'It's too far north for her.'

Conn thought again for a minute.

'Try Lough Nafooey.'

Again a swirl followed by 'She likes Lough Nafooey but there aren't many men-maids up in those Connemara mountains.'

'Men-maids?'

'Yeah, I think she might be done with men for good. She wants somewhere that has a nice selection of men-maids nearby.'

Conn shook his head, not quite believing he was expected to account for the dating future of a mermaid as part of his calculations.

'Oh sure, yeah, you can never have enough fucking men-maids sunbathing around the place can you, whoever the feck they are, please ask her to forgive me,' Conn answered in mock indignation.

Truth be told, he was starting to quite enjoy the experience. Fionnuala's eyes flicked up at him pleadingly and so he settled back down to the task at hand. He thought of all the lakes and some of the rivers he'd visited, but none seemed likely candidates for a mermaid. Finally, he thought of a place he'd not yet visited in the flesh. The lough was rich in terms of Irish history and archaeology, but its men-maid situation was as of yet unrecorded and unknown to Conn.

'Run Lough Gur by her ladyship.'

There was no reply from Fionnuala and, after a couple of minutes, he glanced down at her a little anxious he'd made a mistake and somehow offended the Lady of the Lake. Eventually, Fionnuala beamed a grateful grin back up to him.

'Lough Gur is acceptable.'

'Stocked with plenty of men-maids?'

'Enough.'

Fionnuala removed the stone from the waters and gingerly climbed back to her feet. She scampered over to Conn and gave him a tight hug of gratitude.

'Well, I suppose your work is done here then,' Conn said.

Fionnuala stepped away from him with a sudden gleam in her eyes. Conn looked at her with a new curiosity.

'I think I should take a swim in the lake to celebrate.'

The air temperature was sub-zero and Conn was beginning to freeze just standing around. Both of them were well wrapped up, but Fionnuala's feet were more than a little blue from immersing them in Lough Derravaragh for the duration of her work. The pit of sadness Conn felt earlier was returning along with an inexplicable fear and an anger that seemed not entirely his own.

'I'm not sure that's a great idea, Finn,' he responded with a calmness he didn't feel.

'Oh, I'll just pop in for a minute or two. I'll be in and out in no time,' Fionnuala persisted.

She began unbuttoning her jacket and removed the woolly beanie protecting her head and ears from the elements and threw it to the ground.

'Tell me, Finn, did the lady say anything about who chained her to the bottom of the lake for an eternity?' Conn enquired, as innocently as he could.

'Oh yes, it was Malachai, a man. They were in love, but he cursed her as I suspected. But, thankfully he also cursed himself in the process,' Fionnuala replied.

'So his spirit is still knocking around here somewhere, possibly?'

Fionnuala stopped removing her clothes for a moment to consider the question. Conn took this opportunity to gently guide her into an embrace and he quickly wrapped his arms around her shoulders before she began removing any more of her garments and whispered another question into her ear.

'Why did he place a curse on her?'

The warmth of his body sent a shiver of heat down her spine and she rested her head into his chest, forgetting about the lake for a minute.

'Would you believe they fell out over the water? Malachai wanted to perform a Christian blessing on the waters to protect her, and the Lady of the Lake scoffed at the idea, pointing out the waters were already blessed and protected long before any Christians arrived.'

'Is that right?' Conn murmured, while massaging the small of her back and encouraging her to continue.

'And sure, look at him now, his spirit wandering the fields crying over the beautiful swan that he cursed, like some kind of, some kind of…'

'Spastic,' Conn said, finishing her sentence helpfully and helplessly.

'Maybe, I suppose. You know I don't like that word though. So, you think it's a bad idea to swim naked in the lake?'

'Why don't we investigate the trees and sit down and rest for a while first—it's been a long night.'

Fionnuala bent down and started retrieving her clothes scattered across the rocky shoreline and began putting each item back on until she was re-wrapped as snugly as before. Conn took her hand and placed it in his own, and Fionnuala led the two of them into the wooded area. Almost immediately some brambles began scratching at Fionnuala. Conn swiped them away and picked them off her clothes. Soon, they found a small clearing in the wood and lay down together on the grass. It was cold but warmer than the lake, Conn supposed. Fionnuala snuggled into his shoulder and draped an arm over his chest. He could feel her tiredness and she soon fell into a light sleep.

Conn waited and peered up through the branches at the moon flickering in and out of view. It was casting shadows intermittently throughout the grove of trees and bushes. Conn cast his eyes to the right and watched as the shadow of a bramble started inching down towards the earth and began sneaking along the undergrowth towards him. It looked weirdly like a cross between a lizard and a snake.

'Hello, Malachai,' Conn intoned with a quiet voice, careful not to disturb Fionnuala. The shadow stopped and Conn felt a sharp fall of fright in his stomach.

'You won't be finding any replacements to wear your ankle bracelets around here.'

Conn was remarkably calm and certain considering what he was attempting to do—channel the spirit of a dangerous man. But he had a hunch about something. Conn felt his insides churn again, but this time with the unholy rage of another. Conn closed his eyes and tried to concentrate. A vision appeared and he could see a young man talking with St Cuarach. Pleading with him for a blessing prayer to protect the waters surrounding his land.

'You never mentioned the Lady of the Lake to him, or told him you were going to pray over Lough Derravaragh, Malachai. He wouldn't have given you that particular blessing had he known the details. He was well-versed in the happenings and the enchantment spell cast on the Children of Lir. There was deception in your heart when you uttered those words. Have you any idea of just how much pain you've caused?' Conn scolded him aloud. His own words now a struggle to get out.

After a time, tears began to well up in Conn's eyes and spill down his face. Salty with grief and deep with remorse, Conn felt. The river of tears flowed and flowed down his face, but he didn't know what to do with them or how to process them, and he began shivering with sadness. Because of his clear vision of Malachai and Cuarach together, Conn now felt certain Malachai was from his own ancestral tree. But all he could do was lie and wait until he could think of something to do. Unexpectedly, Fionnuala squeezed his chest tighter and drew Conn closer to her. She was mumbling something in her sleep. Both Conn and Malachai abruptly froze.

'The Lady of the Lake feels your sorrow, Malachai, and she wants you to know there's forgiveness in her heart for you. It's time for you to leave this curse, this gnarly spirit and place behind too now. You've both spent more than enough time chained to its enchantments.'

Conn waited and breathed slowly in and out. Soon, the river rushing down his cheekbones abated somewhat to a stream and then at last to a tiny trickle. Conn could feel the last few teardrops had traces of joy and gratitude mixed into them. And with the last tear the shadow of the bramble completely disappeared from Conn's view.

Fionnuala stirred and opened one of her emerald eyes and looked up at Conn and gave him another squeeze.

'Now, that wasn't such a hard night's work after all, was it?'

Conn started laughing uncontrollably. Fionnuala always had a way to find the right words at the right time.

'True, maybe we should take a skinny-dip in the lake to celebrate.'

'No, Conn—sure only a spastic would consider jumping into Lough Derravaragh on a freezing cold night.'

And with that, Fionnuala closed shut her opened eyelid and fell back into a peaceful slumber. Conn began humming the song from the car and left it in charge of the mermaid-less portal. Then he gradually closed his own sleepy eyes too and off they both went to some other time and some other place.

The Well

The woman said she felt guilt and that a holy well held her—in a well waters embrace. Tiny, wet eruptions of emotion quivered on her tongue and tingled the back of her throat as she spoke. Old jolts of memory; new tears trembled on her lashes. 'The holy well held me,' she said again, and I believed her.

On the drive home from east to west I eased my foot off the accelerator and dipped a toe into the waters. Into dark pools and wells of grief. Miles and miles of Impressionist countryside jogged by the windscreen. I knew a well, and I wondered if she might hold me for a moment or two. On my last visit, I had never thought to ask.

I rolled Brigid to a slow stop on the grassy bank and slid down my window. I glanced across the road to the field and to the holy well. It was cold and blustery and darkish-grey in the heavens. The old St Bridget's well was protected by a circle of trees. I opened the rusty gate and, mercifully, the place was empty.

I bent down on the last step, cupped some water in my hands, and wet my lips. The water tasted a little indifferent. Under some bushes, folding chairs were stacked away. I plucked one out, flipped it open like an umbrella, and sat. I opened my book at random and read the poem I landed on. The wind whistled and whispered through the branches, as it always seems to do here. I could feel my racing thoughts starting to jog, then slow to a quiet shuffle. I lit a rolled-up smoke and considered it for a moment before inhaling a drag of its devilment. I could smoke here all night, I thought.

Beyond the well waters were five trees—four green-leafed and one in the middle, a purple sycamore with leaves of a deep purple hue. A stain in the sea of green. The branches of all five swayed back and forth together as the tempo of the wind rose a little. The deep purples flowed and flamingoed with the greens. An intimate, knowing dance. They seemed comfortable in each other's movement even as the winds swirled around them.

I inhaled, exhaled, and understood the picture in front of me—for it was my picture: deep-bruised shadows of grief, secrets, hurts, and pains. The purple sycamore wasn't so big and wasn't so small either, I noticed. It looked a beautifully natural and unique part of this five-tree forest. It struck me that the greens would be lost without the deep purples.

I sat, mesmerised, puffing away, stilled by the sound of trees and breeze against the calmness of the well waters. I started to speak whatever words came into my head and let them gush out through my lips. They flowed easily and pleased my ears. I looked again at the five trees and something drip-dropped into my mind.

I wouldn't exchange my purple for a fifth green tree—I thought.

Soon, I finished my smoke and rose from my folding chair. I emptied my pockets of the tobacco pouch I had carried to the well, placed it in the centre of the seat, and moved the chair under the protective branch of a tree. I tossed the lighter and the packet of cigarette papers onto the seat too and left. You'd never know who might show up some dark night in need of a quiet smoke of contemplation.

I sat back into the car, content, turned the engine, and looked back across the field to the well.

To the well that held me. Just long enough.

A Trip to Calvary

I was lost. Lost and frustrated, and so I pulled Brigid into the nearest hard shoulder I could find on the road. We were cruising the backroads in some sort of illogical loop around Eyrecourt, Laurencetown and unhelpful signposts for Ballinasloe and Banagher. Without actually happening upon the place I was searching for—St Brendan's Cathedral.

Now, before we proceed further, allow me to back up the car a few feet. At present, the Irish outer-world seems to be behaving predictably enough, but with political toxicity levels rising in tune with the devilish algorithms trained on the nation and its digital personality. As a result, I've taken another short siesta from writing about any current affairs for most of this week or engaging with it at all. The break has allowed enough time to get the hands a little dirty with a friend and reacquaint myself with a few days of manual labour, but also a window to squeeze in an adventure of the spirit. So, news junkies can jump off Brigid's bonnet at this point and start hitchhiking back into Lego-town.

Now, where were we again?

Ah yes, lost and frustrated. So, on this day in question, I woke early and soon decided to treat myself to a chilled and serene day of tailgating the intermittent rolling storm-clouds gathering and then blowing by the back window of the house. Literally and metaphorically, to see if any occasional bursts of sunlight might blast through the overcast skies at various locations along the backroads of County Galway. I was hopeful that each dazzling, unexpected ray discovered might bring with it a new insight, and, perhaps, power-hose some overused thinking patterns out of my mind.

After an hour burning rubber which brought Brigid and me through Athenry and then Loughrea, we caught both rain and sun. Then, after a coffee refill for me and an injection of diesel for Brigid—I was pretty certain Himself was guiding us to a holy site in Clonfert. A rather hasty conclusion. Drawn mainly from the notion that I spend quite a lot of time in Clonmacnoise and its ancient monastic environs, but have never ventured forth to its twin-flame Clonfert a mere twenty miles away. Together this pair seems like age-tested spiritual lighthouses to me, directing traffic up, down and across the River Shannon. For centuries. One on the eastern bank with the other on the western side.

Clonfert—and the Church of Ireland cathedral there—has an interesting history. The cathedral site apparently transitioned from a place of Catholic worship to Protestant at some point during the Reformation. The region seems dipped in both religious traditions. It is also the original monastic settlement and area of St Brendan the Navigator.

Suffice it to say, Clonfert is a rich and important piece of early Irish Christian real estate. While all of that might sound quite wonderful to explore, and someday I might return to explore it further, unfortunately, it is secondary to the events of this particular day as things turned out in the end. Except to relay that at the point I was stranded on the side of the road—lost, frustrated and other words beginning with F—Clonfert seemed central.

I was just about to start fidgeting with my phone and Google Maps when I glanced out the passenger-side window and noticed a graveyard staring back at me from across the road. Immediately, two fingers appeared in my mind: one pressed the play button while the other hit record on a 1980s cassette deck lodged up there. The sun was shining again, and frankly, showing off a little bit—if you want the gospel truth of it. There was nothing for it but to get out and investigate. So, I stepped out, crossed the road and observed a sign on the entrance wall. I rustled up another eyebrow raise.

Hmmm. Calvary Cemetery.

I opened the gate and slowly ambled in and down the centre aisle. I glanced left and right at the common Irish surnames littered all around. The Kenny and Flaherty tribes topped this graveyard poll and for a good few generations back, as far as I could tell. I made my way down to the end and could see clearly now why this burial ground was so named. Calvary and Jesus on the cross.

Now, I know this will sound a little strange, but Jesus on the cross looked quite magnificent in this quiet rural setting. I've never considered the crucifixion scene as magnificent before. The sun was sparkling mischief down on top of my head and I was certain any slow learners present were kind of meant to maybe learn something here. Although, for the life of me I hadn't a clue as to what.

After a time, and a prayer or two, I made my way back to the car and wondered about my own personal journey to Calvary.

Don't we all have to make one? Or do we?

I sat smoking and thinking about this for a minute and I suspected I did. I suspected further I wasn't inclined to sprint towards mine. Had I started this journey and halted or even turned back?

Had I turned my back to Jesus?

I don't mind admitting that of the Holy Trinity—Jesus is the one I relate to the least.

God—yes, Holy Spirit—check.

But thoughts of Jesus are often quickly followed by thinkings of the cottage industry of ancient to modern day religious practices built up around his name. But it occurs to me now that sometimes it's easy to forget the Son of God was a man. And I can relate to a man.

I considered Jesus anew for a few minutes. Set against this backdrop of sheep, cattle and the solitude of a rural Irish landscape. I thought about Jesus the flesh and blood man. The man who died on a cross at Calvary and of how painfully slow it must surely have been. A monumental level of suffering endured with only a sea of jeers and mockery to draw comfort from. You'd want to be mightily sure of the love you have for mankind to entertain such a thing, wouldn't you. Cast in this light, Jesus is quite magnificent to behold.

Soon, I departed Calvary, started back on the road once more, and resumed the hunt for St Brendan's Cathedral. At that stage, I had absorbed enough to understand that the day's destination point had already been reached. The sun continued shining in through the window as I drove, but still the cathedral eluded me. Eventually, an answer stirred within me. Not to the location of the cathedral but to an indecipherable question whispered through the sunlight.

'I'm not strong enough,' I confessed to myself quite truthfully and to anyone else in the vicinity who might be asking questions. I repeated it.

Strong enough for what, though?

The words surprised me a little, or maybe they didn't. Strength is often misdiagnosed or undetected in the modern world, I feel. It often builds from not completely breaking in two when every fibre of your being is screaming to give in or to never get back up. A little burnt oil began leaking out of my eyes. I had an answer to something, and at some point, maybe I'd figure out the question or series of them it was answering.

Perhaps.

Before too much longer, I stumbled on the quaint, untouristy and rather splendid cathedral of St Brendan. I mooched around the grounds and headstones of what looked to be different generations of dead, honest-to-goodness Irish Protestants. One gravestone took my breath away and forced me to stop. It marked the grave of a little stillborn baby. Forty-one weeks. Two words etched on the cold stone pierced me.

Born still.

I'd never considered describing a stillborn tragedy by reversing the placement of the words. Born still. An infant born perfect. Too perfect for the codology of this world and so moved swiftly on to her place in the next one. The cathedral grounds were empty too; the same as Calvary. The cathedral door was locked, but I wasn't too bothered.

In one of the boundary stone walls was a gap between the stones. The crevice was home to a long red candle. I picked it up, lit it and found that it burned long enough for the duration of a single prayer. It is not my custom to offer up prayers for my own needs, but today I allowed myself the indulgence of an Our Father. Then, I exited the site.

I sat back into the ever-patient Brigid, lit another cigarette, and flicked back through some of the photos I had taken at Calvary Cemetery. I began to understand why I took one of them now.

Directly across the road from the cemetery, and right where I parked Brigid, was a most beautiful field. A tillage field. Land resting wild before the excitement of the summer or autumn crops ahead, and perhaps not yet sown for the growing season. But temporarily filled with spring greens and yellow flowers. Or perhaps the flowers were corn marigold or something like that. The scene looked quite spectacular and appealing in its own peculiar way.

I noticed from the photo that the gates to this field were wide open and seemed an open invitation to passers-by to walk on through and take a look around. Instinctively, I hadn't, though. Instead, I'd hopped back in the car and kept motoring on, searching for the cathedral.

But I guess if I'd stopped long enough to think about it, and looked at both sides of the road, I might have seen that beyond Golgotha is somewhere divine. A special place for those who summon courage enough to beat a trail through their own personal Calvary where the heavenly gates might be open wide and welcoming.

The words 'I'm not strong enough' vibrated again, though, and I soon drove away.

Brigid and Frankie Go to Hollywood

I've been tinkering around with the notion that mind mesmerisms can be processed into love. The sales pitch for this spiritual idea commences with a man on a factory floor feeding a few raw materials onto a production line. Inputs such as useless, repetitive, digitally trained thought patterns. Then, after a short hop, skip and jump down to the end of the line, he catches some purity of feeling and connection with mankind, and love purrs off the magical moving carpet and falls into his lap. A little private grá factory drip-dropping good energy into the bloodstream and beyond onto the Irish countryside.

The base materials to begin a trial are simple enough and pretty inexpensive: a middle-aged Peugeot 306 named Brigid, access to a couple of 24-hour petrol stations, general sleeplessness, ample glimpses of the moon, and just the faintest hum of Frankie Goes to Hollywood stretched out on the back seat of the car, singing away in his sleep.

I should offer up a warning, though. Since clinical love trials have commenced, Syria has fallen, Georgia is suddenly on the brink of civil unrest, the Irish government has been re-elected en masse, and Brigid was kidnapped by the cops for non-display of car tax. Now, on this latter line item, I did try to reasonably point out that a man can't very well be expected to display something he doesn't fucking possess and never had any honest inclination to purchase in the first place. But unfortunately, this was not an acceptable defence, and no amount of love potioning could avoid payment of the Brigid ransom down in the Liosban Business Estate to the moonlight robbers and highwaymen.

All of which is to say—I'm still ironing out some experimentation kinks on this idea at various points on the M6, M17, and M18 on a nightly basis now that Brigid is back on the road. But I am hopeful of eventual success.

Two lines in Frankie's 1984 song 'The Power of Love' strike a chord no matter how many times I spin-cycle them through the old eardrums. First, the association of the words 'death-defying' with the word 'love' strikes me hard for some reason, and then, further on, in another part of the song, the line 'let yourself be beautiful' hits just as deep.

How many people genuinely think of themselves as beautiful, I wonder. Maybe one or two percent, if that—never mind the audacity of putting an action verb beside 'beautiful' and, by so doing, allowing themselves the luxury of inhaling and exhaling in this world as an altogether beautiful being. Yet I suspect most could be this and more if we could just fully grasp that beauty is an inner feeling to be embodied more than a perfect image to be found on Instagram. And what a world that might be, eh…

'The Power of Love' is traditionally thought of as a romantic love song—or at least it was by me, traipsing around teenage discos in Dr. Duggan Hall in Corofin at the tail end of the 1980s—but, lyrically speaking, I think it leans more towards a divine insight on love, unconditional love, with its repeated focus on the soul.

'Cleaning my soul… Purge the soul.'

I do like to think of tears as a cleansing agent for the soul, as in the verse above. But also as a sliding-door moment from mind to potential connection with the eternal. The divine is mixed in there somewhere, with all the tears, I believe. My head has always been an ever-blasting hurricane of random thoughts, ideas, aggravations, and easily triggered turmoil. Negativity outweighs positivity a lot of the time. Illusory thought patterns easily spark into emotion, which is my single greatest worry about the electronically sabotaged world. Digital thinking manifesting in mass physical volcano eruptions.

Lately, I've been trying to observe my artificially induced negative emotions. An attempt to examine how a tweet, video clip, or some other piece of tech junk is affecting me. So, when one of these emotions arises and I happen to catch it in action like, say, bitterness, I try to trace it back to the source. In a worrying number of cases, the source isn't in the physical world. But instead of labelling it an emotion, I am trying out a substitute word. And that word is demon, which kinda grabs and focuses the attention in a way a mere emotion does not.

Approached this way, I can say that my smartphone invited the demon into my life. However, what is more troubling is the bitterness or anger demon might then leave the door open for three or four more demons to sneak in of their own accord. Ones I have little or no conscious awareness of, as they aren't triggering the primary emotion. The longer the door is open, the worse the eventual outcome. That is a problem on a personal basis but on a much deeper, societal level too. A particularly frightening issue if the thought pattern established was digitally induced, because I suspect the algorithms planting the seeds are only introducing demon A to hardwire demons B, C, and D into our psyches too.

Anyway, on the night of the big wind last week, I decided to bring Brigid out on the road for most of the storm to see if we had any spiritual issues to iron out after our forced split. To put each other through our paces, so to speak, and seek some divine wisdom. A few worrying episodes recently have brought up nightmarish visions of a life without her, and I was pretty certain I'd brought on this police impounding business not just in the physical realm but in the spiritual one too.

Somehow, someway.

So, we drove down tree-lined backroads, up into the Finny hills, and met spontaneous, magical rivers erupting and flowing down the byways. Fallen branches and bushes bent sideways. Nature's Hollywood, in other words. At one stage, we stopped on the empty motorway and I climbed out to take pictures of the Lego-town signage warnings and orange electric dots—reminiscent of those early pandemic nights in 2020, when all you'd meet on the motorway were a couple of foxes and digital demons telling you to go home. Snaps taken, I hopped back into the car and gradually understood that, in a sense, I was looking to be hit by some turbulence from above on the most turbulent of winter days. A signal from the heavens that I was on completely the wrong road.

But none came. Outside, the trees swayed, the rain lashed, and electrical wires swung back and forth from poles like giant skipping ropes. Inside, there was quiet, a deep peacefulness, and the gentle murmur of Frankie's voice with Brigid's determined engine humming along. I can't remember exactly what I felt those last couple of hours of the storm.

Death-defying love, perhaps.

The Wood of the Whispering

I don't usually remember dreams. I'm not someone who sleeps exactly but rather the type of yahoo who falls into occasional comas of exhaustion. However, about a week ago, a daybreak dream snapped me out of my slumber, and I managed not to forget it. It was a simple enough snooze fantasy, nothing too dramatic. Without getting into specifics, I'll just say this: I dreamt I was observing something happening on my laptop—monitoring a specific sequence of events unfolding. Slightly unnerved, I got up, flicked on the kettle, and made myself a cup of coffee. Then lumbered out into the backyard and lit a cigarette.

I love the tranquillity of early mornings but rarely see them. When I do make the effort, my reward is a clear, empty-ish mind for a couple of minutes. On this day, the key to ignite the engine of my racing thoughts had not yet turned over. I had enough headspace to consider my dream scene slowly and at leisure. Still, I couldn't escape the uneasy feeling that the movie my subconscious had conjured up would somehow find a way to play out in my conscious world.

Most people's dreams, I suspect, are gloriously incomplete and quite utterly bananas. Mine was no different—and in addition, two important questions were left unanswered. The when and the what.

When would it happen?

And what would I do?

A day later, at about 1 am—on August 8th, to be specific—the when question was answered. I suppose you might say my laptop delivered the signal and answer. A number of times. A few minutes later, the what question was also answered, through different means, but again my laptop was the conduit. That unnerving feeling returned. In a sense, I knew the truth of the situation by my reaction. Suddenly, I didn't want to know the answers to the two questions now that I was in possession of the information. Or at least I seemed to be.

So, let's recap. A certain series of small events was going to come to pass, and I knew when these events were going to happen and exactly what I should do. The events did happen—so, cue celebrations, right? A milestone reached and flaw eradicated in my evolution as a living man wandering the earth bumping into things. Right?

Dead fucking wrong.

Over the course of August 8th, I somehow managed to do the exact opposite of what needed to be done. I totally and rather grandly fucked up my dream when presented with it in reality. Cue rage, not celebration. The engine of my mind went turbocharged and wouldn't have looked out of place at the starting line of a Formula One race. Looking back, I can see I had faith in the dream right up to the point I needed to do something about it. Or, in other words, I lost faith at the very moment it became apparent the small vision might be coming true.

The following morning, I woke none too early, but the sun was shining bright—which is to say, I was in good form and not thinking too brilliantly. I determined to try and recreate the events from the sleep cloud I'd botched. This endeavour turned out just about as disastrously as you'd expect.

Now, my dream had a very specific detail indicating the endpoint. After forty-eight hours, or thereabouts, I was close to reaching it for a second time. Again, failure beckoned. While I was waiting to be put out of my misery, I began to reflect on everything—on every misstep and conscious decision I had taken, and whether, in actuality, the dream was merely an indicator of my approaching full-on descent into a permanent state of craziness. My mind was all over the place, but one thought struck me hard and kinda stuck. Maybe the dream wasn't about the outcome of the events themselves, but about my faith. I say this because shortly after chewing on it, and wondering if it might be true, something truly remarkable occurred.

Himself showed up.

I'll repeat that—as much for myself as for anyone reading this— the divine showed up. And showed up in a most interesting manner. He appeared at the very moment when my man-made dream was about to burst into flames and die. Not a centimetre, but a millimetre away from the finish line and failure. On arrival, all He did was hit the pause button. My rational brain cannot find another satisfactory answer to describe it—and believe me, it has tried and will probably continue to try. But the interjection was so very precise, so elegant and obvious, as to defy any other possible explanation.

Himself afforded me a brief window to think. No—let me rephrase. Himself afforded me a brief window to stop thinking. A reminder that I can't think or read my way into belief or faith. Maybe others can, but I can't. All I can really say is that sometimes I randomly feel my faith in God and I was being invited to feel it once more. That's it, and end of story.

Now, this pause seemed like a test of sorts. As if I was being asked, ever so gently, to sense my faith and stop accepting the randomness of it showing up. Or else I would stumble over this same hurdle once more. So, what you might say here is this: I wasn't being guided as to what to do or how to do it, but was afforded a tiny divine window to figure it out.

I often come across YouTube videos about the act of surrendering. Just surrender, they sagely advise. At which point, my overriding feeling towards the creator of said video is to sincerely advise them to go fuck themselves. Then, go outside, light a cigarette and shoot myself in the balls.

How do I surrender my thoughts?

It's not like my mind—or anyone's—has an identifiable off-switch. If the key to my faith and belief is largely switching off my mind, it is going to be a long road ahead, my friends. Anyway, I took my divine intervention into the sitting room along with a cup of tea, two spoons of sugar, and a smoke. I tried listening to some music, but it was manufacturing comforting thought patterns rather than shutting down my mind. The only other option was to go for a drive, so I did, and ended up in a forest on the Slieve Aughty hills up near Woodford in South Galway—a place I'd never been before.

A problem with a lot of forests in Ireland is the gravel paths—I find. The squelch and crunch of pebbles underfoot sometimes make it difficult to connect with the earth, surroundings, and nature. This was one such forest. Although it does seem to be some type of hybrid place—half working plantation with the tall Nordic conifers, and half recreational, with the more deciduous families of Irish trees also growing and on view. After fifteen minutes, I came upon rows of sawn logs stacked neatly on the side of the path—ready to be unleashed and transported into the economy. I looked up to the left, and I could see a motorway-width felled strip where the trees had been chopped down. With the trees removed and converted into logs on the path, I could see these trees (now logs) had been planted on an embankment which rose to a peak height of maybe a hundred feet. I began a conversation with myself.

'I'm not climbing that fucking embankment.'

'Ahhhh... Yes, you are.'

'Do you ever just... like... fuck off?'

'Not really.'

About ten minutes later, I was at the top of the embankment and even managed not to break any ankles on the climb up through the brush and undergrowth. I veered off to the left and began exploring the hidden treasures of the forest. Before long, I found a tree that was pleasant to observe. At the base of its trunk, it was a single tree, but from about two feet above ground it became two. I horsed out my phone to take a photo and found myself having to back up a few steps so as to capture it in full. I inadvertently reversed into another tree, and when I looked down I could see it had a mossy mound dotted with three-leaf clovers. A great place to park my backside, I thought, and no better man to take a lunch break from doing nothing than my good self.

In fact, when I sat down, I found I could quite easily and comfortably lie back against the butt of the tree. I looked up and viewed the forest canopy of branches and foliage around me. In the thick of the woodland, the tall, thin trees were branchless until they raised their emerald bonnets to the sky. From my vantage point, it seemed each slender-framed tree was the same until they reached the canopy top—at which point each tree revealed its own unique face and head of hair. My mind started to relax just looking at this hidden sight of nature, and soon I tuned into the wind gently and almost noiselessly whistling a song through the leaves of the uppermost branches. About five minutes after sitting down, I promptly fell asleep.

I'm not sure how long I slept—probably no more than fifteen minutes—but when I opened my eyes, the woodland céilí music was still in session. I didn't move and merely resumed listening and feeling the music of the birches, the oaks, the pines and the other forest trees that I had no name for. After a few minutes, or maybe more, I had my first conscious thought—which was an observation that I was struggling to entertain any thoughts at all. Soon, the sun began blinking through the trees, as if to confirm His presence—and mine too.

Later, I flipped open my laptop. My series of man-made events and interventions attempting to simulate my dream turned out perfectly. In truth, I wasn't surprised.

For I had felt some faith whistling through me in the melody of the trees.

Divinity between Cell Towers

One of the successes of the last twelve months is how little news I digest or write about nowadays. My modus operandi for scraping together current affairs sentences is a little non-linear, to put it mildly—and becoming more non-linear by the day. Allow me to elaborate.

The most widely read piece I've written over the last three months was an article on mobile phone towers. The genesis of the idea came, out and about, with Brigid during Storm Éowyn last January. We're frequent flyers up and down the Tuam to Gort motorway, all hours of the day and night, as many will know. Anyway, while observing the storm carnage, we noticed something simple but strange.

Tuam had signal, and so did Gort after the storm. But, from about a mile outside either town, I couldn't pick up a wireless signal anywhere along the motorway. Nowhere. Not at any point. I tried several times on several journeys.

Why?

Now, probably some technological reason for this anomaly exists, but I thought it quite odd. Odder still was my disinterest in unearthing an answer to my own burning question, and my inability to listen to music while driving. Instead, a different question emerged into the picture-perfect, still waters of serenity that is my mind space.

Who owns all of these 5G masts peeking in over the dual-carriageway every couple of kilometres like a line of fucking peeping Toms?

And figuring out the answer to this question became the foundation for the article that followed. My hunch was that the controllers of these Irish towers might well be familiar international companies where small concentrations of global cunts like to gather and own everything.

Alas, bullseye.

Now, regulars to this little saloon will have already guessed that the mention of Brigid's name means we will not be driving on a strictly 3D highway for the remainder of tonight's entertainment. The introduction, though, is a good segue to somewhere else. Brigid spells adventures of the spirit, but mobile masts have some relevance in this sphere today. I suppose you might say three discernible realities are alive within me at the moment. Well, I say discernible, but I often struggle to recognise which of these worlds I'm locked into at any given moment—or what combination of them.

Physical reality, the day-to-day synergistic melding of nature and human nature, seems altogether changed. Once upon a time, it was here in the physical world that a spiritual nature could be discovered, trialled, and developed a little more freely. Spiritual signposts, often gift-wrapped for leisurely opening and absorption. You might notice the divine in the unexpected hearty salute from a passing stranger met along the way, or in the snatched observance of peaceful, methodical, and melodic diligence of a neighbouring bachelor cocking a field of cut hay. The wristy strength, the sloping back, and graceful sword flicks of the two-pronged fork, the silhouette building his hay-domed way to the heavens. More ethereal than a black-crow audience scavenging the trimmed meadows for worms might have you believe.

Yet, into this old turf, the cyber intrudes—with the random, frightful force of a blight on the summer's crop of spuds. And I, like a gaunt, half-starved farm labourer, seem little able to protect my tiny fields of rented conacre from its influence. Dig and dig as I might, this infected ground threatens to serve up only the watery, rotted flesh of an Irish Lumper potato.

So then, my search must begin again—or tune in anew. A search for blackberries, wild garlic, nettles for soup, or a gooseberry bush or two. For streams stocked with the salmon of old knowledge. A hunt for my wandering, restless spirit—the third realm—on a road cobwebbed with intricate threads of ones and zeros. It seems a more difficult and distracting treasure hunt, but then again, when I lived in an era of less difficulty and less distraction, I was blind too and circling the same roundabouts over and over again.

Can I use the tools of the new age to access the old one?

I don't know for sure. But I possess a car, of frequent mention on these pages, and she's where I try to bring the first two worlds together with my third. The Brigid realm.

It is here that I listen to music and podcasts and attempt to train my intuition to the seen and unseen worlds around me. She is the place where I pray and the companion that steers me to wild, vast places of quiet reflection. It is where I dream and nightmare. Some days, the four seasons of an Irish day beam and beat through the windscreen and mirror the same seasons all wrestling within me. The big emotions and the no emotions. These escapades have been both blessing and curse; I am, in a real sense, addicted to them, and at this stage of living I'm not sure how to negotiate the outer or inner world without them. Yet, I have a deepening sense that I will need to figure this out in the future without Brigid.

On dark nights, she guides me through the shadowlands. She idles while I take a piss on the side of an empty road, her engine steadily humming as she patiently waits for cool wonder and chilly awareness to encloak me, so for a fleeting moment I might discover freedom at the bottom of a coffee cup of profound aloneness.

But the sun shines too, and often blindingly so. I don't always get this mix of the three worlds correct, but sometimes I do. Sometimes, I ditch the digital altogether and occasionally tech doesn't seem to hinder. But, more and more, a digital unrealism bleeds into this realm of mountains and men nowadays. Disfiguring and altering my perception of it, as if the planet itself can only be consumed at a short remove from a length of cable plugged into a car socket designed for my cigarettes. There is a weird bastardisation of the pandemic era at play in the world now. A kind of inversion of the two-metre social distancing rule applies. Please remain within two metres of your assigned digital asset or electrical appliance.

For the greater good, obviously.

So a passing satellite or some appropriately selected band of not-punk-rock radio frequencies might keep a watchful eye and bathe you in its sweetly seductive vibrations. After all, it is mightily important to remain a programmed consumer of the networks, and not a clear-minded, open-hearted absorber of the wild secrets floating in the winds and rooted in the earth. The whispered wisdoms still rustling through the branches of the fallen forest trees, or the illuminating truths sliding down shafts of sunlight, one after another.

Never mind the ethereal poems hopscotching between moonlight and shadow of an early spring's night, waiting patiently for someone to notice and breathe them in—and then puff them out into the world.

I put down the auld phone recently and picked up an old famine book. Soon, my eyes feasted on the news of an old, hellish storm. January 6th, 1839—the night of the Big Wind, they called it. The harbinger of a decade of sorrow. Ten thousand landlords owned the land. I ponder the number—are things so different now, I wonder? Not many saw what was coming ahead, or had the means to prepare. The people with means often didn't care, and maybe pretended not to notice. But smiled, condescended, looted, and continued on.

Are things so different now? I wonder again.

An anonymous line floats out:—'Faces sparkling with mirth are not the fittest mirror for reflecting the sunken eye and gaunt visage of despair. It requires a heart as well as eyes to be affected by the wants of others.'

It means something, I feel—but not just yet. I'll need to find another blind spot between cell towers to figure it out.

Everybody Knows

Summer is early and everywhere. The West of Ireland trembles with lustful growth—for what seems like forever now. Perhaps it will all end tomorrow, or the day after that, or maybe never. The mountain grasses grow with speed and raw aggression, like they're on a secret mission to overthrow Galway City by the June bank holiday weekend. Wishful thinking, lushful thinking.

The endless can end quite abruptly in this neck of the West. So, I've been trundling up some of the Burren's hills and the mountain ranges of North Connemara. Cruising along backroads in third gear in the hope of finding second. A season of weather designed for short sentences and grassy streamside naps. Parts of the West are gloriously empty and immense and now paint-brushed in streaks of sunshine.

I've been searching for peace within myself along the winding roads. It evades me, though. Like a chunk of ham from a deli roll lodged between two back teeth. I can sense it's there, but can't quite dislodge it with my tongue. Frustrating but not calamitously so. Peace comes and goes like the summer dragonflies whizzing around a Connemara peat bog. But I remind myself it is summer and I spend a lot of time buzzing around Connemara so…

I'm a divided house—upstairs in the mind much of the time recently. And not downstairs at the hearth lumping sods of turf into my heart. I'm hard on myself but soft on myself too. Last night, I tried to get to Lough Nafooey before sunset but just missed the setting sun sinking below a mountain. I was disappointed, but consoled myself. There would be other sunsets. Of course, I had missed the turn for Finny, and by the time I realised the error of my ways and turned Brigid around, it had cost me a sunset. But it wasn't too bad, really—still beautifully coloured, dipped in an afterglow.

Every time I hit the right indicator at the top of the main street in Clonbur, headed to the mountains, I can feel the tension in my neck and shoulders ease a little. My mind relaxes as I absorb the reality of leaving the world behind. And as soon as I pass the football pitch on the right, the Wi-Fi signal usually starts to melt away, and then a few moments later the digital world goes kaput altogether. Alone with just the breeze shooting through the window for company.

Yesterday, the evening sun was massaging my forehead too, and so I lit a rollie. The rollercoaster of giving the damn things up continues. Again and again. A couple of days ago, someone revealed to me the reason they thought I smoked. I listened carefully, as not many offer an opinion, usually.

To cope with grief.

No one knows the answer to this question. Except me—and not even me. So, I was shocked and laid bare by the correct and simple analysis. Afterwards, I spent some of the night remembering the first grief moment. The crutches and the quiet tears and the grief. The wrecking-ball grief. Knowing the dream was finally over.

The first big one killed stone dead in its tracks. Then, ripping open ten Benson & Hedges on the bus. And smoking and smoking and smoking away the tears. Silently, intensely—one after another. Until I could lift my head and fake a smile. And tolerate the world of ordinary things passing by the window. On crutches in more ways than one. The grief wasn't just for the ending alone but for all the times I casually neglected what I loved. A deep, sad reflection and emerging truth—I didn't chase down what I loved hard enough.

And there it was.

Gone.

In a flash.

It's amazing how someone can observe such a truth about me from a distance. Hmm—how many others know, I wonder. Everyone, perhaps.

I smoke for many reasons now. A nice paragraph or pleasurable thought will do the trick. I'll amble out to the kettle and treat myself to a cup of tea with two teabags and then walk outside and look up at the sky and smile and smoke. And exhale.

I could do these things without a cigarette, I suppose. But, for the hurts too bottomless to breathe out, I still like a little something within arm's reach to inhale. So as not to buckle in two, I guess. As I did the first time. So the internal battle continues.

I probably don't need them.

I don't.

Maybe I do.

And the cycle continues.

Anyway, back to yesterday's mountain roads and a thought train of a differing, slowed-down nature—possibly related to my grief bubble above. It began gently wrestling with me, or maybe even pleasuring me a little. As a result of this enjoyable distractedness, I missed the damn right turn for Finny and the black-and-white signpost marked:

Sunset 15 km →

Now, maybe it was the mountain air, or the relaxed smoking, or the peace beginning to simmer and slowly pervade within, but two words struck me hard. Two words from a Leonard Cohen song.

Everybody Knows.

I remember a similar experience months back when the phrase 'You're not strong enough' hit me out driving. I didn't really pass much heed on those words after I wrote them down, but I can see now, looking back, that I could accurately rename the four weeks following that piece of writing as: the month of divine opportunities to get fucking stronger. As one thing after another seemed to go astray in my life, and with Brigid in particular.

So, we shall see what Everybody Knows means for me in the fullness of time. Something or nothing. The outer world is turning strangely at the moment; ordinary people seem to be questioning previously unquestioned patterns of thinking— 'Everybody knows that the dice are loaded,' as old Leonard might croon.

Anyway, as I wheeled the car around in a U-turn to chase down the sunset, another light-bulb flickered on. An addendum to my original thought.

Everybody Knows—Everything.

Vibrationally, the truth is everywhere. It is unavoidable, isn't it? I wonder what will happen if—or when—the energy rises to an unavoidable level. What will that scenario look like, the tipping point?

So, how long can enough people keep shovelling Everybody Doesn't Know Everything into the world and keep the fantasy merry-go-round spinning? At the moment, that world seems to end at the top of Clonbur, in County Galway. About fifty yards up the street from the Centra supermarket.

Seems hopeful enough.

Last Monday afternoon, I was lying down on some headland near Doonbeg, half-looking out at the Atlantic Ocean and half asleep. I had a hoodie doubling up as a pillow beneath my head. About twenty yards behind me was a grassy path that walkers could follow to do a loop of the headland. It was sunny and busy with a mix of tourists and locals out walking. Soon, the sound of birds and the waves overwhelmed me and I closed my eyes fully, allowing me to drink in everything through my ears. Then, suddenly, it began.

Eh, the sound of podcasts and incessant news.

Every few minutes, their AirPods' sonic boom invaded my senses before their footsteps. Almost every passer-by was listening to something and I was surprised none seemed to be listening to music. Or very few. No, by the tone and rhythm of the noise, almost all were listening to serious words on serious topics. I think we might be fooling ourselves—a little—into believing everyone is ensnared by just state television and local radio. A lot of people are trying to tune into a different signal.

So, I suppose, the culmination of my three half-day trips out into the wilds with Brigid isn't much. Distilled to its essence, it's this: Everybody Knows.

Leaving aside the vampiric energy sucking the truth out of the world, we might say the following: Everyone knows old truths are no longer solid. Everybody senses something is up. Or else they wouldn't be so consumed with such serious things walking round one of the most beautiful spots in the world, during one of Ireland's most beautiful summers. They fight the same struggle I do: to tune out long enough so I might tune in.

All are searching for a truth. Some a confirming truth, some denying a truth, or more still avoiding the truth of the world within and without. But we are all in the truth business, it seems to me. On the road back to Clonbur from my missed sunset, I had a last unfiltered thought rising in blue-grey spirals of smoke. Ireland is a divided house. Each bed and head divided too, but not fully yet a den of thieves. People are starting to stutter a couple of common truths, methinks. It is slow speech and indecipherable at times, but words are forming. Hopefully, these vibrations are stirring the ancient within like the slow air of an old sean-nós verse. A song long forgotten—but one Everyone Knows.

The Inauthenticity Killer

The changing tick-tock of the clock discombobulates me. But I must again use that word. *Usually.*

This year, I look ahead and around and feel not autumn or winter, but spring in the air. A surprise and oddity to me. I suppose I've grown more comfortable with the oddness of the world, and the oddness of me and my place in it. Earlier, I snoozed by a lake—nothing too fancy now—just five or ten minutes stolen from the tyranny of Lego-town. With only a pair of carefree swans and a trinity of haphazardly moored boats for company. Plenty enough life and boat room to pause and juice the lungs for the road ahead. Lough Nafooey always seems suspended in a different season.

I lay down and stretched on the empty beach and closed my eyes. I observed the madness of my thoughts as they sped by—one after another, after another. Some, like motorcars at the Indy 500, going round and round. My thoughts, quite frequently, are all vying for attention—and loaded with dangerous emotions as well. Sometimes, I need a seat belt more for the couch than when I sit into Brigid.

Just to settle down and stop fidgeting around the place.

But I'm getting better at emptying the bins, I think—and I'm hopeful of a winter of spring mornings ahead despite the times we live through. Fortunately, today, as I sifted through some old thinking, a sheep, somewhere high up on the hills, bleated out and pierced through my mind-babble. The sound was quickly followed by a faraway dog barking out in protest at something or other. Then, the lapping of the stillish waters and whizzing of some indeterminate insects rowed in behind these two sounds.

Unexpectedly, there was no noise, only sound. My thoughts—an observable feast of nothing particularly useful—sank slowly to the bottom of the lake close by. Drowsiness misted me.

'I'd love to fall asleep here'—my last drowning thought. And so I did, for a minute or ten.

I do love the browns and browny-yellows as they fight with the last greens of autumn. Looking around, it occurred to me this place has not changed for thousands of years—and probably never will, much. The magnitude and depth of it are immense. Too immense to be defeated by any age of man, no matter the superiority cloak he attempts to wrap around himself or in himself. As I stroll, I wonder if nature is the ultimate inauthenticity killer. The pulse of the words pleases both my mind and senses. So, I decide to keep it alive and deposit it into the boot of the car for the return journey to Tuam and to examine it further at a later date.

The plentiful furze bushes fight the shadows and the winter to the death around these parts. Their yellow flowers fallen in many spots along the ground. But the hardy few fight on—still defiantly radiant on thorny green branches. The sun smiles down its approval and encouragement on this balmy Hallowe'en day.

After an hour or so, the urge to stay and the urge to go began their duel. I fished in my coat pockets for my phone and cigarettes, but both were above on the road in the lap of Brigid. I compromised with my internal wrangling and decided to retrieve them and to come back to take some photos and sit on the sandy bank for more quiet reflection. On the way back, I spied the newish gate blocking the entrance to this place for a second time—and on this occasion, fully comprehended the profundity of its meaning. The steel and lifeless gatekeeper looked faintly ridiculous against the backdrop of nature's mountainy autumnal majesty.

But it works—and works too well at discouraging entry.

Hmmm. That is the inconvenient problem, isn't it? Gates and gatekeepers provide a function. It doesn't take much to nudge people into looking the other way or not at all. The goal, perhaps, isn't to stop everybody, but to stop just enough. The iron is sufficiently imposing to encourage the passer-by to trot along and walk a different path or drive a different road.

'So long now, and don't come back!' the steel gate whispers to me.

Yet, it's these gates I must strive to kick open.

PART 4: THE GREEN MILE

I Can't Move

Part 1

An intense four days boils down to three simple words.

I can't move.

I don't mean in the literal, physical sense, but in a more deadpan, Micky Flanagan–type manner. I can go out, but not out-out. If you know what I mean. And you probably don't.

Brigid is history, and my driver's licence is kaput. Curiously, I was prepared for the first but not for the surprise of the second. A series of setbacks on the road over the last few months, including four flat tyres in a row, gave me a sense Brigid's time with me was drawing to a close. I was trying to avoid the inevitable, which is never a bright idea. I consoled myself with the notion she had other rear-view mirrors to guard and guide, and other sinful hands to chance slapping her on the dash. The tale of my disqualified driver's licence is an ongoing investigation, which I hope to return to in future.

So, I can't move. Hmmmm.

Immobility reduces the world to a daily perimeter scope of a couple of miles of shoe leather. For the foreseeable future, at least. It is a test—not a driver's test but a divine one.

Another fucking one.

Hot and heavy, the questions seem to arrive this year. From the heavens and in through the letterbox. Down by the river in town, I try to console myself quietly. Sure, a few of them must've been passed; they're all different, aren't they?

Four days and three words.

I can't move.

A slow-flashing amber light, but not the full red. Or so it feels, after four days and three words.

A divine pause.

Breathe in, breathe out—for as long as it takes. I take another steely breath, and then another, and imagine proceeding with caution and without her. Careful to look both ways for what's coming next.

Hmmm. Maybe I can move.

Little by little. Step by step.

Maybe I can move differently, and sure and slow. Don't these times demand it?

I must stay close and figure out why.

And so I will, so I will.

Yes, I can move.

Let the image turn from mind to matter—I'll find some peace in the clumps of nettles.

Part 2

The world's grown smaller, yet expands too. The initial shockwaves have retreated a little. I discovered an isolated stretch of old road in the middle of town leading out into the heart of the countryside. The Green Mile, I've taken to calling it. Just me and nature on foot.

Everywhere I walk, I bump into butterflies fluttering about and tending to late summer business. Alone and in pairs, mostly. I spied a group of them partying away in the back garden of a derelict house. I stood and stared as they happily floated and whispered through the air above the grassy overgrowth, and breezed lazily from flower to flower.

'It's butterfly season,' I thought. I had totally forgotten butterflies had a season all to themselves.

A little later, I bought a copybook in town and drifted down to The Green Mile for an evening stroll, hoping I might catch a puffy white cloud or two with my pen. A stream runs parallel to the dusty path. I've never seen a stream that wasn't in need of a raft built of tree branches and empty barrels and wild places to go.

Eventually, a cloud sailed by, stating: 'Not everyone who makes you laugh is trying to make you smile inside.' Not sure what it means or meant, but I recorded it in my little brown notebook.

I made the turn and fell into step with my old, white-bearded friend from Lahinch Strand—and my imagination.

'Your head's fierce tanned since we met last, where have you been?'

'Just pounding away on this stretch of road with the palms of me hands and closed fists.'

'Good, good,' he said, smiling.

He nodded his head a couple of times and then pointed up to the top of the church steeple peeking above a thistle of evergreens in the mid-distance.

''Tis a holy day, you know.'

'It is if it 'tis,' I replied with a sigh.

I glanced over to him for some further spiritual guidance but alas there he was—gone. The Green Mile will be home until the lights turn green, I guess.

A Random Conversation

I'm ten days between worlds now. The challenge, if there is a conscious one, is to lose my marbles. Well, to lose my mind without actually losing it entirely, obviously. A tricky proposition but a worthwhile one, I feel.

I've been terrorising the lane a hundred yards from the house with my shoe leather since the loss of Brigid. The Green Mile as previously mentioned. It's a private road leading to the solitary residence at the end of the grassy avenue. Today, I met the owner out on patrol in his car. As he approached me, he slowed, stopped and rolled down the window.

'Is that your coffee cup left up there on the bench?' he enquired, cheerfully enough.

I looked off into the distance trying to remember how many coffee cups I've left on his concrete sofa over the last few days. I concluded the probability was high the cup was mine and chose not to lie.

'Ah yeah, probably. I'll pick it up when I get up there.'

The truth broke the ice. So, we lit a couple of cigarettes and had a lively twenty-minute conversation. He lamented the occasional skulduggery erupting on The Green Mile after dark, and I was content to mostly listen and nod. We were agreed on the declining state of the town in general, especially over the last couple of years. We were also of the same mind on the exact causes of this creeping disintegration, which improved my mood.

My new friend informed me that the county council, which manages the public park in the town, is actively discouraging dog walkers from walking their dogs in the park. A post–Storm Éowyn directive, apparently. One side effect is increased foot and dog traffic on the man's road. As a result, the privately owned Green Mile has inherited an overflow of the public park's dog-shite. As good a metaphor for the state of the nation as you're likely to find.

I had the devil's own job of deactivating my Facebook account this evening. A decision I made three days ago—a self-imposed thirty-day directive that took 72 hours to implement. I suppose I am afraid of missing updates from something or someone important. At any rate, it's finally done, and living in real time will have to fill in the digital gaps. I'm developing a slower rhythm and writing almost daily now. I haven't left Tuam since the death of my driver's licence.

A kind soul has invited me to climb Croagh Patrick—Ireland's holy mountain—with him next weekend, and it's one I might take up. I'm in better physical shape to tackle it this year, I think. I've been scribbling thoughts in a copybook each day, and one is a prayer I've been working on for *Himself*, which I might try while scaling the heights—or the depths.

'I surrender to your will, kicking and screaming in protest right to the very end. Filled with nothing but empty promises, pride, and sin. I can't find my way. Please help me and light the path ahead. Please fill me with your love in my hours of weakness, and I will not forget to love you during my hours of strength.'

'

The Dampened Nettles

Darker clouds rolled in over the last day or two. I'd been expecting them. Often, I can be fooled by two weeks of dry roads and the warmth of the sun's shine. Not fooled, perhaps, but a bit too cocksure of the predictability of the road ahead. Not this time, though. I'd been waiting patiently—maybe distractedly even—for some new showers of rain and stealthy greys to breeze in, to see how I might react to their arrival.

The vibrant nettles seem muted by the wet of these rains. Their stinging leaves, heavily cloaked and weighted with dampness, curiously make their imminent danger more obvious and less worrisome. Dense nettles, but longing for the return of the sun to sharpen their spikes and armour them with the invisibility cloak of lazy surprise. So they might needle a sting into unsuspecting wristy soldiers reaching for a blackberry or fistful of flowers.

The long grasses droop too, hiding stones and tree roots underneath, but the brief heavy showers add thick lustre to their green manes. Heavy with absorbed wetness, they're a reminder that these fleeting paintings are best observed and admired at a distance—without the Wellington boots on. Flickers of sun advise caution: don't trip before autumn arrives. A scene not to be missed—when greens turn to reds, and browns and golden yellows.

I sit on the cool bench and sing an old song under my breath that's playing on my phone. I look down the long, empty lane to my right to see if any are following. But I am alone. This day no different than all the others on this stretch of The Green Mile. I am unclear as to why more don't walk this path, but I've never minded my own company. Aloneness is not loneliness, and I am energised by it when I don't over-drink from its water-trough.

I suppose I could get up and amble back along the lane, back into the busy town, and silently submerge into the noisy din of the crowd. Strengthened with the nourishment of the last couple of weeks, and begin again—with half a smile and half a heart.

I could do that, so I could…

I have done it before, too many times to mention. With half success.

The wispy curl of cigarette smoke itches my eye and draws my gaze left. Once more I consider the high gate and security fencing that mark the end of The Green Mile. What's behind those gates, no one really knows. A house, and fields, and a stream that threads on and on. But not certainty, that's for sure. Beyond the fence lie twists and turns—and more dampened nettles too, probably.

And yet, my heart will only smile at the thought of clambering over it.

Track Machines of Intimacy

Part 1

Late last week, the track machine moved in on The Green Mile to dredge the stream. After the summer's growth the waters are slowed by reeds and rushes. Floating sweet-grasses sunbathe in the current of the stream, swinging their narrow hips, while their slim ankles anchor their movements to the river-bed dance floor. The mechanical beast sits quiet by the river's edge, the day's work done. It rests before resuming in the morning to clinically scoop out more overgrowth. Each day, the metal tracks inch further and further up the riverbank, restoring water flow and releasing stagnancy.

Or do they?

On one hand, these watery islands of green rushes provide natural filtration and purification services, but on the other, excessive growth of the same reedy lads can affect water quality and flow, and degrade oxygen levels as they decompose. The scene is a picture of machine and nature trying to figure things out. However, something jars with the image, perhaps nature's overwhelming disadvantage in the face of the machine's steel feet, iron bucket, insensitivity and lack of subtlety. It cares not for water quality or oxygen or restoring balance but merely remorseless progress up The Green Mile while shovelling giant pails of dead grass on the riverbank.

I shuffle by and photograph the memory.

All week, the potholes fill. Rain bursts fight with the warm sun for control. The dark weeping clouds bucket tears down on top of the rural landscape and the summer potholes transfigure into winter puddles. They please my eye to observe, yet are topped up with hidden danger now too as their innate depth or shallowness is veiled by the heaving cries of the sky. A careless step, a broken ankle.

These holes pock-marking the road are brushed in a sandy brown and my search for a clear pool of water to gaze into ends in failure. The unpredictable wind and frequent showers mean much sediment swirls excitedly around in the darkening puddles as the turn of season whistles and ripples across the face of them. The particles breast-stroking happily in a different reality for a while but muddying the waters. I dip my runnered toe into the icy cold of one of them to stir the pot a little. Maybe someday, on some sharp, chill morning of still sun and icy frost the potholes will calm and I might peer down into one and face my reflection. Perhaps chancing to forget the man staring back and continue on walking reborn.

Behind me, out on the streets and down in the smartphone reality, the glitches in the matrix are everywhere. It is almost the only thing people silently nod and hypnotise themselves on nowadays—the glitches in old universal truths. Something is awry, and five thousand euro bikes and face-lifts can no longer transform the unnatural into the natural. Is this age of laser-removed eyebrows beginning to raise an arched, grey, pencil-lined tattoo where a wild, bushy eyebrow used to live?

I feel a slight dawning—a comprehension that while eyebrows are bothersome to maintain, the world residing in the palm of our hands is not just tattooing eyebrows anymore. But, more and more, digitally printing new lives to replace the pale, pudgy arse cheeks squeezed into ill-fitting pairs of Lycra bicycle shorts and ball-hoggers.

Yet, I speak of these people as if I am not of these same people. But, I am. A slight condescension I must work to eradicate within. I played Gaelic football with many of the men and chased around the nite clubs of my youth after some of the women. So, maybe I am the problem—never a fruitless place to start an existential conversation with myself. Slowed to a walking pace, I'm noticing universal peculiarity in the small details of the town, yet privately seething at my reduced circumstances. Certainty and doubt. Doubt and certainty. Old wounds bubble beneath the scar tissue. Old questions too.

Was I good or was I fucking bad?

Why did I get up off the floor and start typing?

Was that good or was that fucking bad?

Why can't I just give in to the darkness of myself, take off my clothes and just fucking skinny dip in the muddy pothole until I drown?

The questions mount and mount and my mind devours them like piranhas in a feeding pool. My eyes are wet from the showers of rain and hauntings of the past and present. I have no answers. I sit down on The Green Mile's concrete bench and smoke and smoke until the smoke clears a little. After a long while I hear a whisper on the wind.

'I will not defeat myself ever again'

The voice is my own. I roll the words around in my mouth and try them on for size. Then say them again. Tears laced with fire burn my cheeks and I taste them hot on my lips. I utter the words again to the fields and the river and the cows peacefully at rest. A little understanding slips into my senses.

There's a furnace within and I need it to fuel me. Desperately need it—but I need to fuel it too. I can't ignore it or fear it anymore as it's all I've got left. I can't turn to it for life-giving oxygen only on the days I'm choking to death unable to breathe. Someday soon, I'll bend down to throw a few lumps of turf and moist tears into the flames, and find the potholes are empty of both. On that day, I'll expire—in soundless anguish and eternal damnation. Himself will shrug his shoulders:

'I was there in the deep red of the flames, but you turned away from my warmth'

This is me when I'm not trying to be somebody else, I guess. I get up from the bench and turn for town. The height of the storm passes. The rain and mucky path squelch beneath my feet and the sound is now music to my ears with puddles as far as the eye can see. I feel a small bit better. A private joke emerges. Maybe the last steps before total calm, surrender and peace are always a tightrope walk across a grand canyon of total madness. If not—I could be totally fucked. Humour is the last defence of my defenceless wits.

Soon, I soak my ears in the music of the funeral ballad 'The Parting Glass' and hum along. A verse seeps into me: 'And all the harm I've ever done, alas it was to none but me, and all I've done for want of wit to memory now I can't recall'—I listen, and listen again. I can feel the words coursing through my veins. The rain and the wind and puddles of memory sing along. I'm saying good-bye to a part of me I don't want to leave behind and it's viciously painful and sweet to the end. 'But since it fell unto my lot, that I should rise and you should not, I gently rise and softly call, good night and joy be to you all.'

I'll keep walking and humming until the rain stops and the tears dry—in case, just in case, I change my fucking mind.

Part 2

There's no fatigue in my legs or mind all day and night. It seems a battle of wills and a pivotal moment. I see-saw between participation in the war and being a mere observer of the drama taking place. I hit the pavement again for a midnight stroll, heading out to the twenty-four-hour plaza on the edge of town, and sit on the outside bench with a coffee, scribbling down a few thoughts into a notebook.

A couple of Brazilian lads emerge into the night air and outdoor decking area through a side exit. Tired and grumpy looking after a night flipping burgers and dousing the great and good of the town in salt and vinegar chips. The rain lashes down in sideways sheets across the forecourt. Too heavy for the Brazilians to even chance running to their car for flight and exhausted sleep. The duo plonk down near me, under the canopy, glumly accepting their fate. Together we watch the rain for a minute before they start scrolling through their phones. They converse with each other in tired grunts but don't look up to initiate eye contact or connection. None of us do anymore, do we?

I feel sorry for them but I'm unsure as to the reason why exactly. A part of me wants to assure them the heavy shower will pass in less than ten minutes, probably five, and a window of escape will be provided by Himself for both of them to escape to their cars and beds. Passing weather never stands still long in the West of

Ireland, and when you get over the sadness of such a thing, it brings considerable joy and peace.

My head and feet call a truce so I just place my chin into the palm of my hand and rest my elbow on the bench, absorbing the spectacle of nature thunderously howling with laughter at man's concrete glories as it grinds the forecourt to a shuddering halt. Since my exile from Brigid, I find I could sit outside Supermac's watching illuminated rain patterns dance across the carpark sky all night long.

The intimacies of this land bring more balm to those souls water-bred in generations of Irish gales and storms than those baptised in the waters of sunnier climes, I think. I feel inclined to ask the two lads if Irish weather troubles their South American souls. I decide against sharing my caffeinated questions with the two buckos, though, and just return my attention to the theatre of the night.

Perhaps, this is the extra douse of sympathy I feel for them. The freezing rain and blustery north Atlantic aren't tattooed into their DNA. The intimacy of Irish weather is alien to them and would be for a couple of generations to come if they continue careers slaving away for Supermac's or some other fast food soul factory of this gluttonous nation.

Recently, I tuned into an episode of a podcast, and a thread of their conversation seeped into my consciousness, demanding scrutiny. One of the two has been living completely off the grid without technology for a number of years. Even watching them interact on my digital lump of metal, I could feel the tech-free writer was vibrating at a much slower, tranquil pace than his friend. It was visible and reminded me of my visit to Lugh and Pomona high up in the Finny hills a few years ago. But, it was a question asked and answered that struck a deep chord within me. The off-grid scribe was asked what the biggest positive gain he'd inherited was from sacrificing the modern world and technology.

His simple answer?

Intimacy.

Intimacy with the food he eats, the water he drinks and the natural environment around him. Bingo, I thought at the time. Fucking bingo. Although not quite sure what jackpot he'd hit for me.

Tonight, I contemplate the trigger of his words and consider my endless walkathon afresh. My day and night are all about intimacy. I think back to my earlier episode on the Green Mile. An internal intimacy, really. Raw, aggressive, throbbing emotions from unhealed wounds submerged in the puddles. But for once I didn't foxtrot or quick-step through them. Rather a slow waltz and careful appreciation of my shadowy dance partner.

Reduced circumstances and my limited ability to mechanically move have forced a developing intimacy with the natural and even unnatural world around me, one slow pace at a time, and I guess that trail leads to a surprising destination. My relationship with myself. No others can move properly until that one improves. Drastically. Hmmm.

Maybe, this explains a little of my rage at the machine too. It destroys intimacy like a track machine scoops living sweet-grasses from the riverbed. Cold, calculated and emotionless. An intimacy destroyer between each other and within ourselves.

I reach for the past in my writing a lot not as a form of nostalgia, per se, but to remember what it felt like to be Irish in those times, to track down some of the succulent juices of Irish community intimacy. How we looked at each other, felt each other, and humoured each other. I'm not searching for a return to the outer world of harsh existence and dark authoritarianism of a melded church and state, but to the intimate language, depth, music, spirituality and stronger pulse of those people.

The peculiar intimacies of place no longer seem to exist as they once did. There is a creeping sameness rubberstamping everywhere. Again, the new adoption of Lycra bicycle shorts and Botox lips might be an outward feature of it. No one falls in love with the lines around their eyes anymore. Even though they are the careful carvings of every anguish and joy of our lives.

When I think anew about my rejection of the pandemic injections, I can see it was the forced intimacy of a bullying state prescription I was railing against in the first instance. A recognition that in the panicky coercion and authoritarianism, a sacred frontier was being crossed. An invisible boundary but a most important one.

The rains halt as predicted, but when I look around the Brazilians are already gone. As I walk back to town I don't quite escape the arrival of the next wintry shower. It is close to 1 am and the back of my jacket is starting to turn a different shade of wet grey from the latest downpour. The local night-club is open for business and a small crowd huddles outside in a queue. I look up and notice nearly everyone is in their late thirties and early forties. Chatty and loud and filled with the joyous release of faux intimacy that liquor brings. I knew it well once and queued outside the same doors once upon a time I'd like to forget. But, I can still feel the faint tug and temptation. All seem quite undisturbed and unnoticing of the falling rain.

'Nobody Noticed the Falling Rain,' I think, looking at them and myself a final time. It might make the perfect title for a novel to explain these surreal times to future generations. The streets are mostly empty other than the crew queueing for the disco. I put my head down and keep walking on the opposite side of the road.

Where are all the young people? I wonder.

Hmmmm. Perhaps, tucked up in bed, glued to Grok or ChatGPT and trying to figure out how to overturn the wild, damaging intimacies and sins of their parents. Hopefully they'll figure it all out for the ageing codger roaming the streets at night. As I edge in the door, my feet are tired and my mind is too—a score draw between the two warring factions.

I'll probably sleep tonight.

A Grá Unconditional

- a short story about love

Aengus was gently rocking back and forth on the uppermost branch of the uppermost oak in the enchanted forest of Doirí Beaga. A casual observer might have noted that Aengus was not a boy yet not fully a man—but no casual observers existed in Doirí Beaga, only the occasional nosy cloud. Close by sat his best friend, Moonface. The two had met on page twenty-three of *The Enchanted Wood* years earlier and were fast friends ever since that childish, excited page-turn. Perched with them were Seán the owl and Saoirse the flying squirrel. Altogether they made quite the quartet of divilment and divinity, known throughout the ancient forest for their adventuring.

Peering down at the world below, Aengus thought it seemed farther away than the possibilities above—which he took as a confirming sign to proceed. They'd made a pact to run away to one of the other worlds in search of mysteries to sleuth, once an obliging cloud hovered low enough to taxi them on their way.

Inconveniently, no cloud was within easy grasp; a sky of bright blue and sun stared unblinkingly down. They were in no hurry, though, so Aengus looked again through a break in the leaves to the forest floor. In a tiny clearing, Brigid paced about on her magic green carpet of forest leaves.

Brigid, a year or two wiser than Aengus, was swinging her sword with practised elegance, beating back an invisible enemy. She was in training to become a warrior of the Tuatha Dé Danann, and so didn't notice the four sets of eyes sipping in her movements. She was, by common consent, the most fearsome and beautiful young warrior in Doirí Beaga. Dark hair fell to her shoulders in waves, complemented by hazelnut eyes. Tall and narrow-framed, her lean limbs were stitched with muscle—seductively firm, deceptively strong.

An ivory backbone tattooed with the marks of the Tuatha Dé completed the picture. It was said she could flash a sword almost as quickly as she flashed the whites of her ivory smile—in laughter or in anger. Unsurprisingly, all the young men were smitten with her—as was Aengus, and everyone else on the uppermost branch of the uppermost tree.

Aengus smiled, plucked an acorn from Saoirse's stockpile, and tossed it down. It fell slowly, twirling on the wind. Brigid felt its tug well before it arrived but pretended not to hear its fall. But her fingers gently gripped the hilt of her sword. Seán hooted as her blade flashed through the air and split the acorn in a single balletic stroke. Brigid turned and glanced up to the acorn thrower, arched a challenging eyebrow and smiled to herself—as if to say 'Is that all you've got?' Then, waved her blade in the air, and made a theatrical bow before returning to work.

As she turned away, a small sadness dialled into Aengus's smile. He swung his feet back and forth distractedly in the air. Moonface noticed, raised an invisible eyebrow at his friend who merely shrugged his shoulders in answer.

Words weren't needed to begin a conversation in Doirí Beaga. Moonface's wide, pale face shifted; his eyes turned the colour of harvest moons—silver-tinged with orange, a hint of warning. Aengus brush-stroked a pair of solid hazelnuts over his own and they began to converse.

Moonface offered the thought he'd been testing. It seemed simple enough but, like many things in Doirí Beaga, was fragrant with hidden depth: Did Aengus understand why Brigid was so beautiful?

The answer felt obvious—so obvious Aengus nearly yelped and fell from the branch. He glanced toward Seán and Saoirse for help, but they'd slipped away. A large cloud crept over the horizon, threatening to smother the sun. It was moving quickly. Aengus was glad it wasn't yet close enough to force a departure.

The cloud finally took the sun, and the light fell a few shades. Brigid's silhouette vanished. Aengus looked back into Moonface's eyes; the harvest moons glowed brighter, illuminating the space between them. Seán and Saoirse glided back and forth between those moons, waving, unhelpfully.

So Aengus reconsidered the question. The Tuatha Dé were a curious people. His own line was ordinary enough—woodland faeries and cranky elves, with basic talents for sun, moon, and stars. Brigid's people were something else entirely. It was said they lived in many timelines at once—warming fires here and dousing flames there.

A memory surfaced: a midsummer night, he and Moonface had hidden beyond the glow of an elven campfire. Tipsy elves had whispered that Brigid existed on five separate timelines beyond Doirí Beaga: wife and mother, warrior daughter, goddess lover, earthly sinner, divine saint—all at once. The common thread, they said, was her grá for impoverished spirits most in need of love. She loved them in whatever form they could receive, and accepted whatever love they could offer in return—no matter how meagre or strange. Often she received nothing. Most did not recognize the gift. Yet she never wavered, nor fretted over her reputation.

Aengus breathed. He focused on the patch of grass where she had stood. Imperceptibly at first, then with gathering force, warmth rose through the shadows. Though he could not see her, he began to feel her beauty radiate up through the trees—powerfully good, more alluring than any appearance. A tear slipped from his horse chestnut eye and ran to the wide beam forming on his lips. Brigid was truly beautiful, and for the first time he understood the word.

Moonface's eyes softened back to themselves and he grinned. Seán and Saoirse settled once more upon the bark. To celebrate, Aengus lasered a horse chestnut toward the cloud blocking the sun. Be gone, he thought. A single shard of sunlight shot over his shoulder and beamed down to the forest floor. Brigid stood there, staring up, stunned by the sudden blaze. Impressed.

Aengus rose and waved a silent goodbye, then turned to a puffy white cloud now parked above. Saoirse hung from its edge as it drifted over them. With a hop, skip, and jump, Aengus caught her bushy red tail. As the cloud floated higher, Moonface leaped and took Aengus's ankle; Seán settled on his shoulder.

As they flew, Aengus looked down one last time and hoped Brigid would recognize him in the future—not as the man-boy he was, but as the ray that broke any clouds darkening her many worlds: a blazing reminder of his love, unconditional. A grá gréine for the woman who loved so many without condition in worlds blinded by conditions and contradictions.

He needn't have worried for there she was sitting atop the cloud, smiling that smile and began pulling Aengus up to join her.

At a Snail's Pace

At night, I lie on the couch and wait for the rush of thoughts to subside in my heated cup of pot noodles. My brain roars in protest as Coco, my ageing Jack Russell, settles down and snuggles into a light sleep at my feet. A neural network of highways offers up some desperate, last-minute distractions for my consideration—hastily throwing up road signs a few yards in front of the brown, rusted gates of The Green Mile. Signage marked clearly with the words, 'Road Closed.'

Sleep comes slow. At times, I can't see the path ahead, and at others, see flashes of it vividly. I've left this town only once in the last three or four weeks and can now barely remember what it means to drive. I briefly wonder whether I could survive without my feet, and then my hands—what about them too?

I breathe and wait and still my mind with the force of two feathers. The feathers—an odd pair of quills—I'd spotted earlier beneath a tree on a spontaneous saunter around town.

'Ah, that's why I picked them up,' a voice in my head whispers.

Soon, with a little feathery tickling, the distracted images and red warning signals flashing across my brow slow down and begin to distil and purify. In the approaching stillness, the lettering on the council road sign blocking the road changes too.

'Road Closed—Local Traffic Only.'

I smile, pleased with myself, and shuffle over the steel cattle grid on the path. I glance behind to see if anyone has noticed my handiwork. But, of course, no one is there except the silhouette of me and the traffic jam of thoughts I left parked at the entrance.

I write because it is the only consistent way I can communicate properly with myself—to set myself straight in a world of digitally infiltrated thoughts and deceptive, seductive thinking patterns. Sometimes, I write to vibrationally let the people I have hurt and loved in my life know it was never my conscious intention. An apology of sorts. Any warmth in the scribbling is drawn from the shared memories we once had. I could just say I'm sorry like a normal person, I suppose. Intentional or unintentional hurt is probably all boxed in the same category by *Himself* and I'm sure the road to hell is just as paved with unconscious intentions as it is with the conscious ones.

I often wonder if the price of an unconscious sin, once brought into the light and then recommitted, comes with a far, far heftier penance than the original trespass in the divine realm. I suspect it might. It occurs to me that I'm traipsing, sorting and typing through the chapters of my life on The Green Mile—chapters I don't particularly want to catalogue, return to or reveal to anyone, but ones I can't fucking stop writing. It seems to be the only thing my fingers will type at the moment. So, for the moment, I just walk, type, and surrender to wherever it leads.

I see a snail on the ground near the edge of the path and instinctively bend down to take his picture. He's black and brown and a little beaten-up-looking. Seems barely to be moving at all. I wait thirty seconds to make sure he is actually moving and not just intending to move. The outcome seems irrationally important to me.

He slithers forward a centimetre, and I breathe out a little sigh of relief.

The Sun beneath an Apple tree

The fragrances of the mind bathe in the calm intensity of a summer sun's final kisses. A maze of tunnelled highways starched clean of their gloom and griminess and windowless tears. As a blaze of golden yellows serenely unpick ancient locks on winter darkened doors, grinning and giggling as they go.

'Hush now, 'tis summer,' they seem to smile at any scalding thoughts desperate to remain hidden or to cower in the wilderness.

The branches of the apple tree bend and sway with the weight of pregnant apples. It is not a day for the vulnerabilities of love or loss but of the possibilities of birth. Some pause to graciously accept the natural charge of the sunlight on worn-out bones and for the strength of the love in the sun's radiance. There must be strength in love, too. A hardy bunch of growing apples told me so. Soon, quietness and light illuminate the hallways. The fragrances of the mind now a fresh, earthy cologne. Every door hangs open.

Bar one.

The last revealed only when all else is massaged in stillness.

Idly, I pick some stray un-ripened apples from the nearest branch and pray my soul will nourish them. I rap my knuckles on the timbered portal. Awkwardly and out of practice. Nervous too.

Inside, Himself is sitting and waiting patiently. Smiling and delighted to see me.

And already eating a juicy apple from the branch above my head.

A Herd of Cows Escapes the Matrix

It was wet, and the sharp breeze was whipping plenty of moisture through the air when I glanced across the stream. I was nearing the end of the outward path, and the vista from this vantage point isn't usually the most visually pleasing aspect of a stroll along The Green Mile. But yesterday was a little different.

About three hundred yards in the distance was the jarring reminder of the concrete jungle and man's footprint upon the earth—the Parkmore housing estate. One of the older estates in Tuam and built at a time when the County Council was encouraging Travellers to settle and stop roaming around the countryside. Never seemed a wise idea to be advising Travellers about anything, let alone settling for less. Rightly, Traveller history carries with it a deep skepticism of attempts to pen them in.

At present, the estate is a mix of settled people and Traveller stock. A working-class estate, I suppose. A couple of fields lie between the stream and Parkmore, with a few stray horses rambling undisturbed in the rushes and a flock of starlings guarding a single hawthorn tree.

However, on the last little stretch of road before making the turn, a different set of fields emerges across the river. This narrow stretch of land runs parallel to the course of the stream and away from the estate. I'd never really noticed the topography of these fields before yesterday—more fertile and agricultural-looking. It was in this spot I glanced up and across.

My eyes were met by about twenty milking cows walking in step with me on the opposite side of the river. We shuffled along together for maybe a hundred yards until we all stopped. My reason for halting was to turn around, for I had reached the gate that stretches across the road, blocking further progression. The cows stopped for an altogether different motive, I think—although it took a couple of cigarettes to figure it out to my satisfaction.

Anyway, I stalled at the iron gate blocking my progress and observed the unusual herd for a few minutes—while sampling a smoky puff. My usual treat at the mid-point of this walk when I'm not planning on camping out on the concrete bench for half the evening.

Now, a brief aside might be useful at this point. A feature of dairy farming is how dairy farmers manage grass. It's called strip-grazing. Put simply, strip-grazing is a method of grazing livestock in a controlled fashion by giving them access to narrow strips of pasture at a time—usually done by employing mobile fences or electric wire. So, a big field might be marked or stripped out into several plots or units of grass. The cattle graze the grass in one plot and then move to the next one and the next. Once emptied, the plot is given a chance to heal, re-energise, and grow some more grass. That's the official blurb, anyway. I'm not a particular fan of this type of farming of grass, as it tends to encourage overstocking of the land with cattle, but I understand why it is employed by the dairy men.

Okay, so back to Saturday evening. After a few minutes—cigarette break over—I turned around and began the townward leg of my stroll. Half hoping the dairy cattle might start following me back down the road. And perhaps, then, I could add them to my daily diet of new acquaintances, which includes a few snails, birds, out-of-season butterflies, and my early-morning and late-evening bat friend. And sure, then, maybe I could really start dreaming by stirring into the pot some of the orangutans flying up and down the motorway. And before you'd know it, a man wouldn't be too far off getting his own circus off the ground and in a position to buy himself a high-quality, counterfeit driver's licence.

Sadly, though, the cattle stood still in place. I kept walking but stopped every fifty yards or so to see if the beasts were getting tempted to join me. They weren't. Eventually, I stopped across from the concrete bench a couple of hundred yards away, lit another cigarette, and looked back a final time.

Sometimes, the correct amount of distance is all that's required in life for a proper perspective on the same thing. From this consideration, I could view the full stripped enclosure across the stream and could also see the cows were still not moving—but not grazing or easing down onto their backsides to rest either. Most unusual. I could also now observe that they were standing around a young sycamore tree—a tree growing out of the stream's ditch.

Then, on scanning the whole perimeter fence line boxing them in, I noticed this odd-shaped sycamore tree was the only piece of green vegetation growing wild, free and uncontrolled in the stripped field. The only natural wildness available to the dairy herd. Supping in the whole calm picture in front of me, something curious floated into my mind.

They're praying.

Giving and receiving.

They, like me, were attempting to break free—to escape the matrix of coiled wires and electricity constraining their movements. All told, the cattle looked like a late nineteen-eighties

Saturday evening Mass crowd approaching a church. Standing in the rain, huddled in a tightish, semi-circular group around the sycamore tree, with the obligatory few laggards at the outer edges of the herd handing round a box of fags and matches.

I felt certain they were communing with a power greater than themselves in some way. The sycamore a temple of sorts—and collectively, in some instinctive manner, the herd understood the simple obviousness of spiritual matters, and much more deeply than I did. Or perhaps ever would. Hmmm. Something to think about.

Anyway, I walked back to town, satisfied I had solved the mystery of the wandering dairy cows. A walk with a moral and a story.

Himself always finds a way through—no matter the type of electronic fencing. All I needed to do was find the sycamore tree growing through mine.

Bogside Brown Bread.

I embarked on a train excursion to find some bread and some peace. A mini retreat of sorts from the well-worn cares of The Green Mile. The bread-man collected me from Portarlington train station and off we went to his secret abode a few miles away.

Soon, the bread-maker let me in on a secret. One of similar magnitude to the need for turf to continue scenting the Irish atmosphere. Bread has memory, he announced. It made immediate and absolute sense to me. Irish brown bread might well be of equal significance to the Irish language in many respects. If not of equal importance, then just one step below it on the Irish ladder of important things to pass on to the next generation. Old wisdom and memories are baked into each rough-hewn slice of Irish soda bread.

Does that sound a bit fanciful?

Well, when you take a bite into a slice of homemade brown bread heavily slathered in butter (the real stuff, none of your spreadable shite), who do you think of?

Probably, you think of your mother. Then, when you chew a bit more, you might also consider another question.

Hmm. Is this bread as good as my mother's?

A comparison test, in other words.

Past visions, culture, and times brought slap-bang into the present. The tastes and the smells are remembrance; remembrance of the importance of them. Obviously, not everyone's mother baked bread or father was consumed by all things turf growing up. More's the pity. Sadly, a sizeable chunk of the grown-up children of these breadless and turfless parents are currently busy destroying the country in cushy civil service jobs screaming about the environment. I should note I haven't been to the bog for quite a while either, so I'd need to get back to basics and ease back on da pontificating in case I end my days in the civil service measuring the explosive impact of cow farts.

Question:

How can you trust people with the environment who can't remember the environment?

Hmmm. Not sure that I can.

Additionally, if you chance a second slice of buttery brown bread goodness, you'll remember that every mother had her own unique tasting brown bread. A family DNA stamp. The more love that went into the making, the better the bread. Generally speaking. Indeed, you might say, every father had a unique way of processing his turf from the bog. No two bogs started and finished the same. The more smoke from the chimney, the more warmth in the home and bread in the range oven.

In the smells and in the tastes and in the sights, Himself was within easy access. You might say, he provided the simple raw materials, all around us, to help navigate a path to him. In the bogs, the breads and the fireplaces. Perhaps, we didn't consider and value them as such at the time. But, sitting here in front of the last dying embers of the night's turf, it seems to me, as a nation, we should have.

With that, it's time to stretch the legs. The night is pushing towards its peak, and the bread-maker's dough will soon be rising with new memories of the past.

Eclectic Picnic

Each day, fast-moving clouds appear and then quickly bluster across the canvas of the Laois skies. My little escape is nearly at an end. The winds have a cool hint of Cailleach, Goddess of the Winds and High Queen of the approaching winter. The sun peeks out, shakes its head, and peeks back in again. Then tries again fifteen minutes later. Fifteen miles away, Electric Picnic draws to a noisy close. One hundred thousand souls—men, women and A.N. Others in attendance, the locals say.

A festival exercise in mass communal belonging, perhaps.

Here, though, on the outer blip of the picnic radar, it is country-roads quiet, with the sky a country black. The vast sweeps of aerial blackness are dotted with a multitude of stars. Rain threatens the days, but there's safety baked into the nights. Or so it seems.

Outdoors, the oak trees are laden with green acorns and the flow of the canal waters swims against the tide of an outside world ready to detonate into thunderous, murderous terror-fields of blood and man-made fire. The rage of the machine cranks up another notch or two. The talk of it is all-consuming to the all consumers.

The swallows, though, have had their fill of bad cess and pack their bags in hurried disgust. In another couple of days, they'll head off for sunnier climes. As they always do and always will. Maybe some year they'll chance to stay if our bad news and bad ways ground to a halt for an autumn or two. Or maybe not.

Yesterday, I sat on a chair to consider the sunrise. Some tall, sinewy trees and evergreens whistled out a tune from a passing breeze. The birds sang and danced to the music of the hastily thrown-together composition. Over and back, high and low, they flew and then across the canal air, like a bunch of drunken bargemen stumbling home after a lock-in at their favourite quayside pub. Exuberant, boisterous, confident—and between you and me—wildly fond of themselves altogether.

For a second or two, I managed to dip my head into the power of it all. The oneness and the belonging. The spirit within magnetised to the greater spirit of nature and natural things all around. Then, like a flash, it was gone. Like the last wisp of a dream caught behind the shutters of opening eyelids. No way back until I might seduce my eyes into a sleepy wakefulness again.

It is a time to belong in this world, yet fewer and fewer remember the way.

Requiem to Jack and the Hop-Ups

Earlier in the afternoon, shuffling along the grassy path, I noticed the concrete symbology of the Waterboys. Black letters marked 'H' for water hydrant and 'SV' for safety valve on a concrete column that stood stern and upright in front of the barbed wire fencing that ran parallel to The Green Mile—separating the lane from the fertile grasslands on the opposite side of the River Nanny.

It's a secret lettering system marking the locations of the water-related pipework and other accoutrements of the town's plumbing. Hinting at the underground network of people keeping the population's thirst and uncleanliness at bay. A bunch of wildflowers grew beside the marking stone, and, all told, the mini scene resembled a headstone and grave. I thought of Jack Hession, the capital 'H' in hydrant. So, I stood for a moment to pay my respects, and the memories came flooding back.

The deep pools of my mind hearkened back to another time and other places. To an age when I was a temporary member of The Waterboys—the County Council version, not the famous Irish '90s pop band.

It was the summer of 1996, and then as now, I was between worlds. Just finished university but not quite sure where to get drunk next. In the absence of obvious choices, I spent the summer working in the county council as a temporary labourer. A position acquired through a little family nepotism.

In all walks of life, rivalries exist, and the sleepy County Council was no different back then. The friction between the road workers and the water gang was mostly good-natured but needled at times too. At the 10 am break, if we were still in the general vicinity of Tuam, Tommy, Jack and myself would roll into the council yard in Tommy's Ford Transit van for the tea break. Usually, a fair number of the road lads would already be congregated around the steel hut waiting for the kettle to boil, admiring a stack of Men at Work road signs, leaning against the wall in a non-ironic fashion.

'Ah, will you look it here, if it isn't Tommy Glynn and the fuckin' Waterboys. Give us a song, lads, coz ye cunts couldn't find a burst water main if it came gushing out of the jacks and hosed ye in the arse.'

Tommy was a fitter by trade and the senior man, a big barrel of Mountbellew good humour, and he'd merely chuckle aloud, accepting the barrage of compliments hurled in our direction without much aggravation. Safe in the knowledge, though, that Jack was growling under his breath somewhere, and dripping with saliva like a bullock landed out of a slatted house after the winter and would intervene with a blast of fucks if things got a little too salty.

The townies were all in the roads section, and Jack, a reformed alcoholic, knew every pub secret in the tea-cabin along with the location of every manhole cover in North County Galway and wasn't afraid to dive down into the shite of either when the occasion demanded.

I didn't realise it at the time, of course, but this turned out to be my all-time favourite job in the history of my life. Mostly outdoors, manual labour, cruising along the country byroads in the van and holding up traffic with a jack-hammer whenever the hell a man might feel like it.

On Monday mornings, the lads would be full of chatter about the previous weekend's Gaelic football matches, drink and the state of affairs with the 'hop-ups' at home. The latter a term of endearment and mild sexism reserved for the good wives of these same council workers. Who, for the most part, back then, were housewives tending to the land and raising the children, while their husbands went off living it up on the highways and byways of the county from Monday to Friday, labouring for the mighty county council. I was pretty clueless as to exactly why the men referred to their wives as hop-ups and too embarrassed to ask.

Generally speaking, the homes where the hop-ups were in charge of cashing the weekly council cheque, which arrived in the post on a Friday morning, seemed the happier homes. By a fair distance. The precise meaning of hop-ups became clear one Monday after a particularly excitement-packed week of burst water mains, extensive weekend roadworks, and wage packets topped up with plenty of overtime gushing through the letterbox.

As a result, the cupboards at home were filled with food and some luxury items alongside a few pounds left over for deposit in St Jarlath's Credit Union. In such circumstances, by general teatime agreement the hop-ups were exceedingly well pleased indeed. So much so, that Tommy and a couple of others launched into soliloquies of their wives' pleasure and good humour and passed the yarns around the hut. Most stories involved accounts of passion frenzied wives grabbing a hold of the swarthy hunk of council meat in the bed beside them and *hopping up* on top of them after Gay Byrne wrapped things up on the Late Late Show the previous Friday night. Lotharios of the Late Late—Late Show.

Of course, the conversation wouldn't happen today, too many taboos for a modern workplace environment. But, I guess why I remember it is because there was a certain innocence to their risqué chatter and a certain pride too that they were men who had wives at home happy with them. The *Fifty Shades of Green* was the cherry and not the cake.

Now, Jack and his wife rather famously detested each other. Tommy would often collect him in the mornings from the house and he'd never leave home without forty Woodbines and about two thousand pounds wedged into his wallet pocket. Tommy ran short of money one morning and asked to borrow a tenner and Jack pulled out the wallet and the two of us nearly had a heart attack at the sight of so many purple twenty-pound notes welded into the old wallet.

'For fuck's sake, Jack, it's dangerous walking around with so much money. You should lodge it somewhere.'

"Tis a lot more fucking dangerous leaving it at home' was his dry reply.

Jack had quit the boozing many years before I arrived on the council scene that summer but sobriety did little to improve things at home. In fact, the opposite seemed to be the case. He was a hard man and spoke little, but when it came to work and getting his hands dirty there was none to match him. I remember one time there was a blocked sewer somewhere outside the town and we were trying to locate different manholes to check the flow of the wastewater, to get some idea about where the problem lay. Tommy and myself were walking up and down the road looking for one but to no avail. When Jack arrived on the scene he took one look at us and treated us to a scowl reserved for a particularly useless pair of spare pricks, then pointed into a field by the side of the road.

'There's a manhole in the middle of that field,' he said.

Sure enough, after a bit of mooching around in the meadow adjoining the road, he was proven correct. Soon after, he was staring down into it with the black Wavin rods, pushing and pulling them back and forth, fucking and blinding and smoking. But before too long the offending blockage was cleared and a steady stream of the town's shit began flowing again.

It was nice to stand in front of the hydrant flowers and reminisce about those times again. Tommy in the driver's seat, Jack beside the passenger door and me in the middle between the two.

Sitting in that strange place I've always sat.

Resurrection of a Driver's Licence

I suppose I found this beautiful stretch of road due to the loss of Brigid, but at the time of discovery I skipped daintily around the death of my driver's licence—a two-year licence suspension just a little over six weeks ago.

Right enough, it was a sudden, shocking predicament to find myself in, which I only discovered when renewing my car insurance earlier in the summer. One irate visit to the courthouse later, I learned I'd missed two court appearances—of which I knew not a jot—related to a police stop and summonses issued well over twelve months ago, and not long after inheriting Brigid from the saints and scholars. Non-display of tax and insurance—the offences in question. This saga had been running non-smoothly since early April and finally came to a thumping conclusion, in my absence, with a full and final two-year driving ban and substantial sum in accumulated fines.

Now, without going into the details, I would say the following: I'd be the type of fella who'd view driving without insurance as a kind of mortal sin, while driving without car tax—well, I might view that as more of a venial sin, if it's a sin at all, of course. Anyway, I was certainly not guilty of both, while remaining careful here in print not to admit to being guilty of any. In my elevated state of fury with the courthouse folk, I insisted on an appeal.

Over the period of the last month, though, I had more or less come to the conclusion that I wasn't going to go ahead with the appeal. Two nights after the startling licence penalty, I got it into my head that I was going to go out for a drive. Fuck them, I thought. Obviously, without a licence, but also without insurance, as it had expired a few days earlier. You might say I was still amped up. However, when I got as far as the car, I discovered it was clamped in a private car park—a first-time clamping occurrence in over twenty-five years of living and parking in this town.

I took the clamping as a divine message, rather than just another one of my numerous parking and road-traffic violations to be added to the list. I'm quite serious about that last sentence.

'You must stay put,' the message seemed to warn.

After a few false dawns of rage and temper, I tried to surrender myself to the driving situation. The discovery of the Green Mile has helped ease me into a surrendering frame of mind and spirit. Over the last four or five weeks, I pretty much decided that I am going to get stronger with or without the aid of a fifteen-year-old Peugeot 306 named Brigid. Indeed, I found myself enjoying the micro-discoveries to be slowly found along nature's way and recording them to memory and in print.

Then, last Tuesday evening, a call came in.

'Do you need a lift to court tomorrow morning? I'm off work—I can give you a lift.'

I had purposely avoided making arrangements to get to the town where the courthouse was located. If I couldn't get there, I couldn't appeal—went my logic. I had forgotten that I'd told my friend about the appeal. But he had remembered.

We made initial arrangements to meet the following morning at The West's Awake's new fifty-thousand-square-foot headquarters on the edge of town—a super structure some people erroneously call Supermac's. After I got off the phone with him, I knew I was getting my driver's licence back. I wasn't elated or excited or questioning or thankful even—just strangely certain. And so it turned out to be.

Sure enough, the offences were struck out the following day. If I was to make a comment about my four or five appearances in the district court this year, it would be to say I'm glad I took the opportunity to defend myself in the public setting afforded rather than engage a solicitor. Curiously, things have worked out more often than they haven't. I am conscious that stating that here might invite in some evil future spirits, and there's a good chance I might walk out the front door and slam straight into a lamppost with a police summons taped to its girth with my name on it.

So be it.

Anyway, after court, my friend deposited me back at the corporate headquarters, where I treated myself to a celebratory coffee and then went for a walk. I shuffled as far as the town park and sat down on one of the benches—one located beneath the protective umbrella of a huge beech tree. Some sun was shining through the branches, and I sat listening to peaceful classical music on the phone, oblivious to the walkers and joggers passing by, just absorbing the pleasing outcome of the day. After a while, it began to rain, but the huge branches and foliage of the tree kept the raindrops at bay and prevented them from reaching me. Soon, it eased off, and I decided to finish out the evening with a visit to the Green Mile.

Before long, I was in front of the rusted brown gates guarding the entrance, my head down dodging the watery potholes, when I glanced up. What I observed next felt like the obviousness of the day's events—the sudden appearance of Himself, showing off a little between you, me and the potholes: a rainbow arching directly over the river and my well-travelled road.

A necessary aerial display to remind any dunces in the pothole vicinity who and what had just happened earlier in the day—the rainbow, a much-maligned word in recent years, restored to its proper, heavenly context. Magnificent and radiant. Small bursts of emotion spontaneously began to bubble within at the sight of it, and I felt the truth of my eyes.

'You're some cunt for one cunt,' I thought.

Long-time readers and fans of Brigid will be surprised to note that I have not yet taken her out for a spin. She needs de-clamping, re-insuring, and half a new clutch, but I find myself in no rush to get motoring. No rush at all. There are roads to be driven—and driven hard—in the weeks and months ahead, but some lessons to be further absorbed at present. I'll keep walking until I get the sign to get moving again. I've learned a lesson or two, perhaps.

Some roads need to be walked, not driven—and walked alone for as long as it takes to get to the other side.

And, of course, another one too.

A friend in need is a friend, indeed.

Parting is such Sweet Sorrow

I wanted to give The Green Mile its proper due. Sitting here now, warming my feet against an orangey flame, I can feel the protective warmth of her recent embrace of me. With a little distance, my mind's eye adds depth and texture to the picture canvas. A palette knife etching deep colours of autumn into those late summer months. A time so long and so short too.

I can see the stream to my left in daylight, and again to my right in moonlight. I can make out the outline of my grey jacket, hoodie and headphones. The view is from behind as the back of my hooded head bobs up and down and all around as I walk quietly along the grassy way. Scanning the contours of the landscape and livestock while at all times tracking my proximity to the safe harbour of the concrete bench and some rest if needed. A hammock of thoughtlessness in a sea of busy thoughts.

Like all bubbles, The Green Mile has burst. The ending was as unexpected and sudden as the arrival, but the memories linger and luxuriate now, smoking the peat-sod air with a hint of earthy fragrance. I smile at my recent self and give him the big salute from a fireside chair. An old dog insisting on the hard road, his furrowed brow oblivious to the silent pleasure and healing his solitary portrait provides me tonight. The overall picture takes me back in time and then back some more.

I have a fondness for remembering what it felt like to be young. Ireland was everywhere and obvious to me in a way it is not today. You kinda have to go looking for it now. Back then, the table had a block of butter and soda bread ever-present and a twenty-kilo bag of spuds in the corner of the kitchen. They're all gone now, and we lost something more than a staple diet with their disappearance. Little losses mounted on top of one another over time.

One of the lessons I learned as a football-mad youngster was about the art of losing and then, much later, winning. As a teenager, we seemed to lose underage county finals every single fucking year. League and championship. As a group, we kinda developed an almost artistic and acrobatic flair for losing county finals. Under-14, Under-16, and Under-18.

Then, after years of losing and heartbreak, out of nowhere, with little or no expectation, we won an Under-21 county final. The average age of the lot of us was 19 years old. So about twelve or thirteen of the team were young enough to play on for another two years and more. This fact had the effect of lightening the pressure. There would be other opportunities.

Afterwards, during the initial burst of celebrations in the dressing room, an emotional throbbing of all those lost finals washed slowly through my veins along with the joys and ecstasy of victory. It was a surprise to find old pain was a huge part of the new prize. The fallen tears and sleepless nights of suffering now tasted like the finest and sweetest of wines. A sensation in my bones that victory would've been less without the old failures.

When you lose a lot in football or, I suppose, in life, a curious thing can begin to develop in the psyche. You start becoming more consumed with avoiding the pain of losing than obsessed by chasing the thrill and hopes of winning. Losing hurts too much. Subconsciously, you try to inoculate and prepare yourself in advance for the suffocation of a future loss, which unfortunately almost always guarantees you'll never see true success. Opening the hurt locker is the surest path to victory, although it's not a straight road paved in rose petals.

As I sit here thinking and typing about my six or seven weeks walking and writing on The Green Mile, a new realisation emerges. I didn't realise how happy I was going through it all.

Until tonight.

Himself and me

Triggers. Emotions. Wounds.

When I think of a trigger, I think of a gun—usually pointing somewhere. It is a deceptive image. Emotions often feel like blood spatter—from the trigger's pull and the sound of gunshots. But the wound is almost always in place before a trigger has been pulled or a shot fired, hidden in plain sight. It's easy to get bamboozled by the present gunfire and completely miss the old wound.

Now, standing on the starting line near the head of this road of mine, and stumbling blindly down this briary path, I found the expression 'Himself loves me' a most ridiculous trinity of words to lump together in a single sentence: a rather grandiose notion to entertain. A trigger. One primarily focused on 'Why would He love me' instead of 'Why don't I'.

I tried the phrase aloud in front of a mirror, not a million moons ago. My body reacted—immediate rejection. I quickly averted my eyes from the man staring back at me in the mirror. It was as if I were attempting to force-feed my eyes a lie. And maybe I was, in a manner. They were only words, after all, and ones infused with little or no belief.

In a way I can't fully explain, I think our bodies are a storehouse for every negative thought and deed committed throughout our existence. So, in a real sense, they contain scar tissue of every dark thought and shadowy deed we've entertained in our lives. In moments like the one described above, the muscles automatically contract and every fibre of my being braces itself for incoming trouble. But the reaction was a starting point and a place to begin a little exploration.

What were the things my body was hauling out from the subterranean depths?

Well, let's just say one or two lines of enquiry vividly flashed before my eyes. The temptation was to merely shrug my shoulders and mutter 'well, I can't do anything about that now, can I?'

Usually, you can though. Inconveniently. Whether it's making peace with those images flashing in my mind or earnestly examining them and maybe doing something about them for future protection.

Now, repeating the exercise of saying 'Himself loves me' in front of the mirror brought some mixed results. Occasionally, on a logical or cerebral level I could believe the words, but in a way that isn't particularly good or useful. Like, you know, on the days when life is going well and I'm feeling good about myself. But good can quickly turn to 'goodness me'—as in, 'what the hell did I just say or do?' Where the inner dialogue speaks with confidence and then, bored with itself, swells into no little arrogance and a few other sweet delicacies.

'Well, of course *Himself* fucking loves me, and actually a little-known fact about my good self is... like... I might be totally fucking awesome altogether.'

Not particularly useful, shall we say. Now, this is when the overflow from my cup of positive feeling starts leaking into my ego and eventually my ego wants to grab the cup and start guzzling it down wholesale. We all need a healthy ego to survive, but I guess we also all need to know when to stop feeding it pints of Carlsberg. And from my drinking days, I know the last pint of lager on a night out should really have occurred five or six pints earlier than the actual last one.

Any brief breakthroughs I've experienced down the old bog road have been when I believed I felt a love tugging at me. Fleetingly. Most often questioningly. An accidental discovery on most occasions.

'Was that him?'

'It couldn't have been, could it?'

When a love-like feeling brings tears to my eyes—and, if it indeed is Him, a realisation dawns—that His love is humbling above all else. The sheer power, intensity and majesty of it. Thunderous and ferocious almost. Thoughts and mental activity are briefly lost, but when they do return I can't help but accept how utterly insignificant and flawed I am, and yet astonished too at how vitally important he's just made me feel. How unique I am to him, how particular his love for me is—and, further, how singular his love must be for everyone.

Not a Yellow Pack or one-size-fits-all type of grá, I would say. Himself, I suspect, loves people exactly in the fashion they need to be loved. So I guess much of the spiritual journey is about figuring out how best to receive this gift as much as it is to offer up praises, prayers and love to him in return. Or how best to honestly accept myself so I'm properly placed to receive this extraordinary munificence.

In these momentary alignments, there is a certain knowledge too that I couldn't cope with more than a few seconds of His focused attention at a time. An affectionate warmth to be treated the way a car treats fuel. It only takes a couple of minutes to fill up the tank, and yet the car might run on that fuel for a week or more at a time. I suspect my path ahead will be made easier then by reducing the number of times I get lost and dragged down the wrong roads between refills. So I'm trying to cut the wrong turns between refills, not arriving at the meeting place desperate, nor getting stranded in a lonely valley on empty. Anyway, these are just a few of my current musings on a topic I—or most men—probably don't give much consideration.

The path ahead is uncertain, but treating it as an adventure is helping—an ongoing attempt to internalise and accept that Himself might actually love me—and if He does, sure, I might as well chance holding the gaze of the man staring back in the mirror. While he might be a cunt, at least he's finally cycling home on a Friday evening with John o' the Hill. To a farmyard where the two of them realise together they were never made of the right stuff to be real bad ones, like.

Epilogue

Brigid was sitting on a kerb in the centre of Ballinasloe town, half on the road and half on the footpath—immobile. Himself was shining in through the front windscreen staring at me, and I was staring back. It was two days after my release from the confines of The Green Mile.

All systems go, right?

Eh, try dead wrong for size instead.

The clutch in the car was gone and so too the gearbox. Earlier, I had visited St Brendan's cathedral in Clonfert and was making my way back to Tuam. I had a reason to go, part selfish, part unselfish. During the summer I had made a promise at a holy-tree there and in a sense my return to it was an attempt to find a way to renege on it. I was looking for another way. I was uncertain and questioning my motives. Were they pure or were they impure?

On the drive away, frustrated, I asked Himself for a fucking sign. Fifteen minutes later he duly delivered me one. So, there we were in a staring contest on a busy street on a Sunday afternoon. A week before the Ballinasloe Horse Fair with him gently explaining he wasn't in the mood for horse-trading. The Brigid era was completely over, that much was obvious to me. But there was more, and it's taken me a month or so to figure it all out to my satisfaction.

You see, he'd given me a book—the one I'd already written over the last four years—but I was too blind to notice the precise nature of it. He knew the over-caffeinated basket of wet turf he's dealing with at the moment wouldn't sit down and write a brand new one from start to finish. He also knew I hadn't really put my shoulder to the wheel to start putting it all together.

I remember that afternoon in Ballinasloe vividly, the stern but patient rays of sun. The tow truck and the final good-bye. The surrender. There were no tears, or rage, or anger, or any great enlightenment. I just got out and walked away. Knowing I was lucky to be able to, and that I was ready to chart a different course. I can see now the breakdown wasn't about the car but about a lockdown era that was fully at an end. But, Ballinasloe was about something else too.

At least one or two of those golden strands of sunshine were reserved for the promises I had made in Clonfert to myself about a little boy named Nicky. I met him and his family during the summer of 2025. Nicky's story doesn't fit neatly into the arc of my journey or this book but maybe on reflection he is the arc and the rainbow in it. What nobody knows, except Himself, is I let Nicky down one night in Ballinasloe. I attended a quasi-political function in the town to try and advance his cause on the quiet. I got distracted and agitated and allowed myself to fail. So, my end piece is a little different to all the chapters that have preceded it in this book. And that's probably just as it should be. Hopefully someone will read it and be a spark that makes the difference.

It's late, the tea is flowing, and the cigarette butts are mounting outside. Old ghosts and old souls sit by my side as I type the last few words. Funny thing, just like The Green Mile, there's a part of me that doesn't want this book to end. The twelve-hour nights and the midnight lunch breaks. Strolling around the deserted town wondering if everything I've written down sounds right. Maybe it does, Maybe it doesn't. But, it is at an end now. I smile as I hear the final words floating by my ears with an updated ringtone.

'Be careful, or you'll end up in Ballinasloe, like The Manager'

Turns out it's not such a bad place to have a breakdown.

Mo Anam Cara

I was parked at the Applegreen petrol station in Athy and called Nick Flood, Nicky Jnr's dad, for a second time to let him know I was close by. It triggered memories of our first call last Sunday and the remembrance of an unlikely serendipity that initial phone conversation threw up. Nick and his partner Nicola spent many years of their life together living in a village called Milltown in County Galway. This also happens to be my home village and the town I grew up in and where I sit down tonight to type these words about a special little boy.

Much later, after we finished up our three-hour conversation at their kitchen table, Nick mentioned he was a bit wary and slow to make contact with me after my initial messages to him on Facebook. Many have appeared on their doorstep before and not all came bearing the truest intentions. As strange as that might sound.

To date, all of the mainstream newspapers have appeared at one time or another and even a small television crew spent an afternoon in their front living room. Fundraisers and charity events have been organised. Some good and some not so good.

A while back, a donated pair of boxing gloves went to auction and was purchased, yet the money was slow in coming forward and the successful bidder paid a second time for the gloves while the situation was resolved. The Sunday World produced an article on Nicky Jnr with a link to his GoFundMe page but many of the mainstream papers never followed up on their initial enquiries. So, Nick was rightly a bit hesitant when I first reached out.

Once bitten, twice shy.

Nicky Jnr turned two years of age on May 3rd. But on his delivery date into this world, every medical professional and consultant in the Coombe Hospital, Dublin, estimated a very low life expectancy for him: a single, solitary day of life—they all advised.

Nicky would die, and die quickly, they promised.

But Nicky Jnr had different ideas. As did Nicky Jnr's parents, and his six brothers and sisters. Today, over two years on, and as I left the family home located in a housing estate on the edge of Athy, Co. Kildare, those ideas were still different to the Irish medical establishment and yet Nicky Jnr is alive and kicking. But his future is far from rosy. Nicky Jnr knows not what tomorrow will hold, but then again, it has always been thus during his short existence on earth.

Born with Down syndrome, Nicky Jnr also has a hole in his heart, requires a double lung transplant, suffers hyperthyroidism and has recently had an operation to deal with cleft lip and palate, amongst other complications too many to mention.

On the plus side, though, Nicky Jnr has soul. The pureness of it pulsating from his eyes as he squirmed and wriggled, full of life, on the kitchen table under the watchful eye of his older sister and then later on as he sat quietly in his mother's arms. Despite the obviousness of his many physical frailties, and the brevity of my encounters with Nicky Jnr on my visit, I was left in zero doubt that I was in the presence of a quite magnificent soul. Indeed, I felt that if all of us in the kitchen that day were stripped of our skin and bones, stripped back to the soul, Nicky's might lift the roof off the house.

But I am racing ahead of myself here and need to slow down a touch to take you back to the very beginning of his story, a beginning that really started around week eighteen of Nicola's pregnancy.

At week eighteen, Nick, Nicola and family were living in temporary accommodation—a two-bedroom apartment in Athy—provided by the McVerry Trust. Now, how the family ended up in this accommodation is a story that will resonate with many in modern Ireland. For it is a story of Ireland's working poor. The barely coping class. People not impoverished enough to qualify for social housing from the housing lists but who try to struggle on in private rental accommodation. However, with each new foray into the private rental market, in recent years, the family were met with higher and higher rents and left closer and closer to the poverty line.

Nick, now a security professional by trade and working nights to support the family at the time, eventually found himself with nowhere to turn after the landlord of their home, prior to moving into a McVerry Trust apartment, asked them to move out on short notice. With Nicola pregnant and facing an extortionate rental market, the family were left with little by way of options. Desperate, and quite embarrassingly for Nick, he was offered temporary accommodation in one of the McVerry Trust apartments in Athy. The embarrassment emanating from the fact it was an apartment complex where his employers sometimes provided security services.

During this section of my conversation with Nick and Nicola, sitting at their kitchen table, I could see Nick visibly struggling through this part of their story: the decision to accept the McVerry Trust accommodation. But with a family and Nicola expecting Nicky Jnr, they had nowhere else to turn. During this period, the housing units left a lot to be desired and the unit assigned to them was filled with damp and mould. But beggars can't be choosers, as they say, and the family moved in. As things turned out, this feature of the housing wasn't the biggest of their problems.

No, not by a long shot.

Approximately two months after moving in, while queuing up to pay rent, Nicola was assaulted by a foreign national living in the complex, and according to both Nick and Nicola, this individual had been kicked out of a number of other residences in the area for partaking in and dealing in drugs. The initial fracas saw this man in an altercation with his girlfriend, and Nicola relates what happened next.

'I went up to pay the rent, and as I was waiting for the change, a girl put a baby into my arms and, out of nowhere, I was thrown up against a wall in the communal kitchen by this Ukrainian lad.'

The baby was the child of her attacker and he then attempted to bite the nose of his own child, according to Nicola. Nick, as a result of his training as a security professional, managed to subdue the man but his own partner was already hurt at this point.

'I went to the staff and told them I was going to hospital and they told me that there was no need, but it was up to myself if I wanted to go. When I got back from Portlaoise Hospital I went to the Garda station but it was closed, so I went the following morning to make a statement. Then, after two weeks, I went back to the guards to see was anything done from my statement and I was told they could find no statement that I had made.'

At Nicola's twenty-week scan of Nicky Jnr in Portlaoise Hospital, and shortly after this assault, a ruptured placenta showed up and with it much reduced blood-flow to Nicky Jnr in the womb. It was also at this twenty-week scan that potential trouble ahead raised its head in the form of medical reports advising Nick and Nicola that Nicky Jnr probably had Edwards syndrome or Patau syndrome—both genetic disorders with high fatality rates.

Edwards syndrome is rare, occurring in about 1 in 5,000 to 6,000 live births. Survival rates are very low: only about 13% of babies born alive with Edwards syndrome live past their first birthday. The outlook for Patau syndrome is similarly bleak. Both feature major congenital deformities, restricted growth in the womb, low birth weight, and major complications post-birth.

Shortly after this, at approximately week twenty-three, Nicola remained in the Coombe Hospital until Nicky Jnr was born four weeks later and thirteen weeks prematurely. The trigger for her move to hospital was in April 2023, when Nicola could no longer feel or detect any movement or kicking from Nicky Jnr. His fight for life was well and truly underway. A fight, one might argue, that the medical establishment did little to aid him with because it was also at this point in his emerging life that termination options started to be consistently dropped into conversation and whispered in Nicola's ear. Options she and partner Nick refused to consider.

What we can say for certain is Nicola fought against any temptation to terminate her pregnancy even though advice suggested Nicky Jnr possessed a condition allowing for late termination. On week twenty-seven, Nicky Jnr was born weighing a little over 900 grams, a couple of spoonfuls short of a bag of sugar, and a new fight for life commenced in the outside world.

'His crying sounded like a little kitten when he was born,' said Nicola.

Doctors weren't convinced of his chances of survival and were reluctant to relinquish their pre-birth diagnosis of either Edwards or Patau syndrome. Each day brought with it a prognosis of imminent death from staff.

'He's probably going to die today.'

Though Nicky Jnr may have cried like a kitten, he seemed to be fighting for his life with the heart of a lion. Day one eventually passed, a key landmark. Then day two came and went. Days three, four and five followed suit.

Little Nicky battled on. Somehow, someway.

On day six or seven, post-delivery testing brought a different set of results and an updated diagnosis: T21, or what is more commonly referred to as Down syndrome.

'We laughed with joy when we heard he had Down syndrome, because it meant his chances of survival increased,' Nicola said.

It wasn't until July 2023 that Nicky Jnr was stable enough to transfer from the Coombe Hospital and thus began the next phase of his struggle for life. On arrival in Crumlin, Nicola and Nick met with their youngest son's multidisciplinary team (MDT). An MDT is a mix of specialists and supports gathered to review a child's complex needs. It was only at this stage that his parents learned that Nicky Jnr had suffered an earlier grade two bleed to the brain, to add to his chronic lung condition and congenital heart disease.

While in the Coombe, Nicky Jnr contracted Covid-19, introduced to the ward by a member of staff, which led to a six-week period in isolation, and in Crumlin one other major incident occurred. This latter incident is subject to a legal case currently in train and so I can't go into too much detail about it other than to say little Nicky developed aspiration pneumonia. Aspiration pneumonia is a lung infection that occurs when a person, in this case a baby, inhales material such as liquid into the lower respiratory tract instead of ingesting it properly. In Nicky Jnr's case, this resulted in severe damage to branches of his already underdeveloped lungs.

When it became abundantly clear Nicky Jnr wasn't quite ready to give up on his life and leave this world without one hell of a fight, a different option began to be mooted. One gently encouraged onto his parents: giving up their child and handing him over to institutional care.

'I'd be crying, and they'd be getting to me on my own, asking had I got postnatal depression and kept reminding me that he was quite likely to die. I was wondering if they were doing it to break me and give up.'

As told by Nicola, frequent reminders were laid out to her as to Nicky Jnr's likely future and how difficult it would be for the family to cope.

He might develop autism.

He might develop cerebral palsy.

He'll never sit up.

He'll never do this, he'll never do that.

All of the incessant and building chatter bubbled to the boil one day during a meeting between Nick Flood and his son's MDT, when it was revealed to Nick that the couple would not be able to take their child home but instead that Nicky Jnr was going to be put into care. Curiously, it was the family's housing situation that was cited as the primary reason. According to Nick, this was as a result of a visit and report on their newly sourced accommodation which reported finding damp and mould when installing facilities for Nicky Jnr in their rented home. It seemed the number of obstacles mounting up in front of the little boy and his family would never stop multiplying.

However, it was at this point something broke in the couple's and little boy's favour. A medical social worker on the MDT gave them the name of a solicitor and urged them to call him. She promised he'd work to find them alternative social housing quickly. Sure enough, within a short period and before his release from hospital the family had secured new social housing in Athy, and indeed this is the same home I visited them at for my interview. So, when Nicky Jnr was finally released from hospital on 8 January 2024, he arrived into a new home with his family and not into care and with a fighting chance of survival. Still, though, his future was very uncertain and the couple were advised as follows during his last days in Crumlin:

'Take as many photos as possible because he's likely going home to die.'

In a sense, this was true. Nicky Jnr was being sent home from hospital but released into a palliative care scenario from the Irish medical establishment's perspective, and while the couple refused to sign a Do Not Resuscitate order the implication was obvious. Suffice to say, investment in Nicky Jnr's future via operations to mend the hole in his heart or receive a double lung transplant in Ireland is close to zero. Hence, the creation of a GoFundMe account to try and source these procedures outside of the Irish State.

So, while Nicky Jnr might still be alive, the hard truth is that the system seems to expect him not to be with us for long, with minimal future procedural intervention by the Irish health system. It was at this point during our discussion that we turned away from talk about doctors, hospitals and medical procedures to more personal, real and everyday concerns. Like how did the couple's relationship suffer during this whole period and how were the rest of their children holding up in general?

'Ah sure, we were gone almost all the time, and there were times when you'd be trying to buy their love with a toy from Smyths. None of it has been easy on them, especially the younger ones,' Nick replied honestly.

Nicola followed on:

'Oh, there'd be times when we'd be telling each other to fuck off out of the hospital room but I knew if we didn't stick together as a team, Nicky would die.'

The rapport between the two of them during our conversation was very relaxed and complementary. Nick is a natural talker with a reassuringly calm demeanour and is quietly persistent, while Nicola often interjected to zone in on a particular episode and clarify specific points with detail. For the whole time I was present, Nicky Jnr was a very real and loved part of their big family and passed between the arms of his mother and the older kids, who are close to being young adults now. This background scene brought to mind another question.

'If I had a magic wand and could grant you one wish to heal one of Nicky Jnr's many problems, what problem would you choose to tackle first?' I enquired.

'I'd love for the hole in his heart to be closed,' Nicola responded, instantaneously.

In September 2023, Nicky Jnr was christened by a chaplain in the hospital and not even this was a totally straightforward process. No doubt, faith in God played a major role in Nicola and Nick's decision-making at every step along the way and throughout the last two and a half years. To my casual eye, they don't appear to have got many of these decisions wrong on behalf of their son. In the days after the christening the area around Nicky Jnr's bed became decorated with holy cards, rosary beads and pictures of the Blessed Virgin Mary along with other memorabilia to mark the occasion. Soon, though, they were removed by hospital staff and piled together on a locker.

'I had his room decked out like a shrine but they wanted them all taken out of his room,' Nicola said.

Nicky Jnr was too weak to be brought even as far as the hospital chapel for his christening, but both Nick and Nicola found great solace in the hospital church throughout their stay and, as Nick said:

'The church was the only place I could clear my head and think for a few minutes.'

The last eighteen months, post-release from Crumlin Children's Hospital, have brought frequent return visits and stays at both Portlaoise and Crumlin Children's Hospital. Nick estimates the number of emergency visits at between ten and twelve.

Nicky Jnr lives on, though.

Breathing in and breathing out with silent persistence.

The GoFundMe account has a target of €150,000 and currently sits at a little over €40,000. Nick and Nicola hope to one day bring Nicky Jnr to a hospital in Boston to have the hole in his heart fixed and possibly also undertake that double lung transplant. But after the initial flurry of media interest and support, the dial has slowly ground down over time. The digital world brings news of other concerns and other places to invest our time, care and attention.

Nicky Jnr smiles and fights on. The little boy with the big soul.

Mo anam cara.

Nicky Jnr's Go Fund Me page

https://www.gofundme.com/f/our-little-warrior-nickey

Printed in Dunstable, United Kingdom